GENESIS

Biblical Commentary
Through Dialogue

KYLE WOODRUFF

Copyright Page

For those who helped along the way

CONTENTS

GENESIS 1-3

ADAM & EVE

The woman whom You gave to be with me,
she gave me fruit from the tree, and I ate.
—Adam

"I'm just not buying it."

"Buying what?"

"The whole universe being created in seven days thing," said the boy. "'Let there be light' and all that jazz."

"I didn't know it was for sale," said the old man, moving a pawn forward.

"You know what I mean," said the boy, sliding a bishop across to take it. "Obviously the Bible has played a major role in shaping our culture, but the stories I've read seem like mythology people take as history." Streaks of sunlight splashed through the trees as he placed the pawn with a small collection aside the board.

The man lifted his knight and placed it in the newly opened space. He whispered, "Check," before saying, "Well, what do you think Genesis is about?"

The boy grumbled something under his breath while he looked over his mistake. "Well, I think it was made to explain our existence, before we had science to learn the earth wasn't the center of the universe and all that. A lot of cultures have origin stories, but now there's too much evidence for evolution for someone to convince me to drink the creationism Kool-Aid."

The old man said nothing, just stared at the board, so the boy carried on.

"But I think the debate over historical accuracy takes away from the positive things the stories have to offer," said the boy. "I'm pro-Bible, let's put it that way. Not a fan of what organized religion did with it, but I'm willing to put that aside and talk about the book itself."

"That's fair," said the man.

A warm summer breeze blew across the park and tousled hair into the boy's eyes. He pursed his lips and blew it out again. "Go ahead. I cut you off."

"Quite alright," said the man, flipping back to the page he was on. "I prefer a dialogue over a lecture anyway. But I'll skip to Adam and Eve. I'd like to hear your thoughts on that one."

"Remind me where this supposedly took place again?" said the boy.

"Well, there's mention of a river flowing from Eden that divides into four branches, so that's our only clue. The Tigris and the Euphrates we know of, so a few suggestions point to the head of the Persian Gulf. That would be southern Mesopotamia or modern-day Iraq. But the Pishon and the Gihon are unknown, so I guess we can't say for sure."

"Alright," said the boy, moving his king out of check, "go ahead. You were about to tell me how God rips out one of Adam's ribs to make a woman."

With a smirk, the old man said, "I think it's laid out a bit more tastefully than that, but that's the gist of it, yes."

"Bone of my bones, flesh of my flesh, and she'll be called woman," said the boy, "or something like that, right?"

"Close enough. Then the next line is just beautiful," said the man, looking down at his Bible to read aloud:

> Therefore a man shall leave his father and his mother and be joined to his wife, and they shall become one flesh.[1]

"And the man and his wife were naked and not ashamed or whatever," said the boy. "But I never understood that line you just read, because at this point Adam doesn't *have* parents, so it doesn't make any sense, ya know?"

"You've got me there," said the man as he took his next move. "I won't pretend to understand everything the Good Book says. This line may allude to the rules of marriage coming down the line, signaling a shift in the ancient culture where the highest allegiance was to one's parents. This verse makes it clear that a man's duty is to forsake his parents and shift loyalty to his wife. Anyway, I just think the description of marriage is beautiful."

"I take it you're married?"

"I was," said the man. "She passed a while ago now."

"Oof. Sorry I brought it up."

"Don't worry about it," said the man.

The boy gave a nod as he took his move and said, "I cut you off again. Go ahead."

So the man read on:

Now the serpent was more cunning than any beast of the field which the Lord God had made. And he said to the woman, "Has God indeed said, 'You shall not eat of every tree in the garden?'"

And the woman said to the serpent, "We may eat of the fruit of the trees in the garden, but of the fruit of the tree which is in the midst of the garden, God has said, 'You shall not eat it, nor shall you touch it, lest you die.'"

But the serpent said to the woman, "You will not surely die, for God knows that in the day you eat of it your eyes will be opened, and you will be like God, knowing good and evil."[2]

"Right, right, right," said the boy. "So she sees it's good for food and takes a bite and gives some to Adam. Yada, yada, their eyes open and they realize they're naked." He reached for a piece and then stopped, rethinking his move as he carried on. "So I have a few thoughts here. First of all, you have to ask, why a snake?"

"You know," said the man, "I never thought to question the serpent itself."

"That's because for someone who believes in creationism, you probably overlooked the evolutionary importance of snakes."

"What do you mean?" said the man.

"Well, when we were still living in trees, snakes were one of the few things that were always a threat. We could hide from crocodiles in the water, lions on the ground, or birds in the sky, but when we were out of reach and hidden by leaves, one of the few things that could still sneak up on us were snakes. They were always a threat to be aware of, so it's fitting one should open our eyes to being vulnerable."

"So that's your take on what being naked means?" said the man. "Being vulnerable?"

"Well, go ahead and read the first thing they do after they eat the fruit."

So the old man read:

> Then the eyes of both were opened, and they knew that they were naked, and they sewed fig leaves together and made themselves coverings.[3]

"Right," said the boy, "they cover up their most vulnerable parts. But in reality, it wasn't a piece of fruit that made us aware, it was the snakes climbing our trees that were around long before this story was ever written down. Think of it this way. The tale of 'Little Red Riding Hood' didn't put wolves in the forest, the wolves were already there. The story was just used to warn us to go in the woods with caution."

The man raised an eyebrow. "Interesting comparison. However, I always viewed being naked as the soul being stripped of its natural clothing, purity and holiness, so Adam could no longer stand before his Creator without feeling the need to hide from shame."

"I see what you're saying," said the boy.

"And from the Christian point of view," said the man, "the serpent is Satan, who baits his hook with the promise of intellectual delights, opposing what God told them about dying."

"Right," said the boy, "the snake is tricky because he doesn't challenge God's authority, but he does make them doubt whether or not God can be trusted. It also hints that God is jealous by implying He doesn't want them to know what He knows. So if what the snake says turns out to be true, we know God's a jealous liar."

"Bold statement," said the man.

"But no one ever *promised* not to eat the fruit," said the boy. "They were merely *told* not to eat it. In fact, Eve wasn't even around when God told Adam not to eat it. Technically, God never told Eve not to eat the fruit. She just heard a rumor after she poofed into existence." The old man laughed as he moved a piece on the board. "But then she adds, 'nor shall you touch it,' which God never specifically said." The boy scratched his head.

"What's that called when you say something you were thinking about but didn't mean to say?"

"A Freudian slip?"

"Yeah," said the boy. "I think it's one of those, expressing her desire to touch what she's not supposed to."

"I guess that could be true," said the man, "but she could have also just misremembered, or added an extra layer to highlight God's command. Whatever the reason, though, it allowed the serpent to play on her words and make God seem even more restrictive than He was."

"Right," said the boy. "Adam, though, what a piece of work he is. He doesn't exactly put up a fight when Eve puts the fruit in his hands. He defies the Almighty almost immediately after God made him. Makes you wonder, was God not very convincing? Did He not come off as an authority? I mean, what reason did Adam have to go against His will? It wasn't like he had a chip on his shoulder where he felt the need to stick it to the Man. He didn't grow up in a bad neighborhood or have mommy issues. He didn't even have the excuse of, 'Oh, were you talking to me, God?' It's like, 'Yeah, pal. You're the only one *here*.'"

"Right," said the man. "His passive behavior is as striking as her eagerness and excitability. Not only that, but the text makes it seem like Adam was nearby when Eve took the fruit, as she didn't exactly have to go looking for him. This raises the question of whether or not he overheard the conversation with the serpent, and if so, why he didn't jump in to stop it."

"I guess we'll never know," said the boy, scanning over the board again.

"Some of us engage with temptation," said the man, "and others follow those who make the decision for us." Then he looked down at his Bible and read again:

> And they heard the sound of the Lord God walking in the garden in the cool of the day, and the man and his wife hid themselves from the presence of the Lord God among the trees of the garden.
>
> But the Lord God called to the man and said to him, "Where are you?"
>
> And he said, "I heard the sound of you in the garden, and I was afraid, because I was naked, and I hid myself."
>
> He said, "Who told you that you were naked? Have you eaten of the tree of which I commanded you not to eat?"[4]

"First of all," said the boy, "if God is all knowing or whatever, why would He have to ask these things? Wouldn't He already know the answers?"

"I believe this is God's way of giving Adam a chance to admit what he's done," said the man, "to repent."

"Mmm," said the boy, nodding his head. "That makes sense."

"But instead, there's an instinct to hide the truth from God," said the man. "Adam mentions why he hid but doesn't exactly mention the disobedience from which his sense of being naked arose."

"Right," said the boy. "Instead, he's a real class act and says, '*She* made me do it!'" The old man laughed. "Rats her right out, the gutless prick. Not only that, but he throws it back in God's face, if I recall. 'The woman *You* gave me,' or something like that, right?"

"That's right," said the old man with a smile. "Avoiding blame seems to be a natural instinct from the very beginning. Instead of taking responsibility for his sin by going back to our loving Creator, Adam lays the blame on someone else."

"And then she blames the *snake*," said the boy, advancing a pawn. "It's like, come on, guys. What are we doing here?"

"And notice how the serpent remains quiet when Eve shifts the blame," said the man. "I heard a preacher once say that a transference of blame is a transference of power. Adam blames his wife, and the dominion shifts when God turns to her. Then she blames the serpent, and the serpent accepts the allegation with silence."

"And you said Christians see the snake as Satan, right?"

"That's right," said the man. "The preacher said this act was how the Devil gained his power in our world. Imagine how differently history could have unfolded had either of them owned up to what they'd done."

"Yeah, that's an interesting take," said the boy. "Then they all get punished, right?"

"Right again," said the man, running his fingers down the text to find his line:

The Lord God said to the serpent, "Because you have done this, you are cursed more than all cattle, and more than every beast of the field. On your belly you shall go, and dust you shall eat all the days of your life. And I will put enmity between you and the woman, and between your seed and her Seed. He shall bruise your head, and you shall bruise His heel."

To the woman He said, "I will greatly increase your pangs in childbearing. In pain you shall bring forth children, and your desire shall be for your husband, and he shall rule over you."

Then to Adam He said, "Because you have heeded the voice of your wife, and have eaten of the tree about which I commanded you, saying, 'You shall not eat of it,' cursed is the ground for your sake. In toil you shall eat of it all the days of your life, both thorns and thistles it shall bring forth for you, and you shall eat the herb of the field. By the sweat of your face you shall eat bread until you return to the ground, for out of it you were taken, for dust you are, and to dust you shall return."[5]

"Seems like Eve got the short end of the stick on that one, doesn't it?" said the boy.

"What do you mean?" said the man, taking his move.

"So the snake has to slither on his belly, boohoo. That's more of an inconvenience, not to mention that's what snakes *do*. And so the man has to sweat a bit as he feeds himself. That was his purpose in the garden anyway, wasn't it? But Eve, man. 'In pain you shall bring forth children' and 'your husband shall rule over you'? If I was Eve I would've pushed back here, like, 'Woah, woah, woah, *God*. You made it clear that the day we ate of the tree we would surely *die*. Pain and being ruled over weren't part of the deal!'"

"There's a description I read once," said the man, scratching his temple, "but I can't for the life of me recall who said it. Anyway, it went something like, 'Eve was made from Adam's rib, pulled from his side to be an equal, not from his head to rule over him, nor from his feet to be trampled over, but from under his arm to be protected, and near his heart to be loved.'"

"There you go with that soppy marriage stuff again," said the boy.

"You'll understand one day," said the man.

"Doubt it. But what kind o—"

"Let me just say," said the man, "that when God made Eve as Adam's 'helper,' it wasn't in this bring-me-a-sandwich kind of way you kids throw around these days."

The boy laughed. "I can't even believe you know about that."

"You'd be surprised what your grandchildren let loose in front of their elders now," said the man. "But the term 'helper' wasn't meant to be a servant. From my understanding, it was supposed to mean something like 'strength' or 'power.' God gives man dominion over every beast in the land, but for man, there was not a matching *strength* or *power* to be his partner. And when God says, 'It is not good that the man should be alone, I will make him a helper as his partner,' what is really being said is that He'll make him an *equal* to ease his loneliness."

"I guess that makes sense," said the boy.

"And sound marriage advice in terms of what to look for in a partner," said the man. "But where she was brought into the world as an equal, she abused her influence in this way by drawing her husband into sin, so God established subordination."

The boy nodded quietly.

"What were you going to say before I cut you off?" said the man.

"I was gonna ask what kind of punishment is death anyway? They barely know what it was to be *alive* at this point. Was it supposed to be frightening? How would they have any kind of instinct to avoid this so-called 'death.' Neither had seen anything die before. Shit, I would have gone straight for the tree too. But instead they're punished, and now our whole relationship with God is based on a lie, or at least manipulation. This is the birth of daddy issues if you ask me."

"I'd like to point out that while they didn't die immediately, in the spiritual sense their sin caused separation from the source of life. And in the physical sense, this decision led them to the slow dying that comes with mortality. Remember, they had permission to eat from every other tree in the garden, including the tree of life, in which case they would have lived forever. But because they chose to eat from the tree they were told not to eat first, He cast them out before they had their chance at immortality. So in the day they chose sin, they also chose mortality, or death."

"Wow," said the boy, "I never would have caught that. Here I thought you were too wrapped up in the story of becoming one flesh, and I'm over here like, 'Fool me with the old death-for-suffering switcheroo once, shame on you…'"

The old man laughed, then he pointed to the board. "I think it's your turn."

"Alright, alright," said the boy. "Finish reading while I find a move."

So the man read on:

> And the Lord God made garments of skin for Adam and his wife, and clothed them.
>
> Then the Lord God said, "Behold, the man has become like one of Us, knowing good and evil, and now, he might reach out with his hand, and take fruit also from the tree of life, and eat, and live forever." Therefore the Lord God sent him out of the garden of Eden, to till the ground from which he was taken.
>
> So He drove the man out, and at the east of the Garden of Eden He stationed the cherubim and the flaming sword, which turned every direction to guard the way to the tree of life.[6]

The boy slid a bishop across the board and a large grin spread across his face. "I think you've got a decision to make."

The man looked down at the board and stroked his beard to consider what the boy had done.

"There seems to be some trickery when God commands Adam not to eat from the tree though," said the boy. "It sends a mixed message when He tells them, 'Don't eat from it, *for the day you do,* you'll die.' He doesn't say, 'If you try to eat it,' He clearly states, 'The day you eat it.' You have to wonder if God planted that seed in their minds to set them up for failure, ya know? Then He could go ahead and kick 'em out of paradise and make it seem like it was their fault, making fear the basis of their relationship moving forward."

The man's gaze remained on the board, so the boy went on.

"He seems to know Adam would hear 'don't eat from the tree' but Eve would hear 'for the day you do,' and she'll see this as inevitable with a why-put-off-until-tomorrow state of mind."

The man moved his castle and immediately the boy slipped his bishop across the board and took his knight.

"You know," said the boy, placing the knight gently to the side, "I heard this rabbi interpret the story once. He said God's intention was to have Adam and Eve go down to the lowest world to do His work. After He brought them into existence and gave them instructions, Adam says to Eve, 'Did God say not to eat it, or did he say someday you will eat it?' And Eve says, 'God is asking us to choose. Don't eat from it and live, or eat from it and die.' Adam laughs and says, 'Well that's a pretty easy choice,' to which Eve replies, 'No, He's hoping we eat it.' Confused, Adam says, 'How do you know that?' So Eve replies, 'Because our job is in the lowest world, and this is not the lowest world. There's a world in which people die, a world of mortality. That's the lowest world, and that's where our job is.' So Adam says, 'But God put us here. That can't be a mistake.' And Eve goes, 'It's not. God brings you to where your job is, but you have to volunteer your service.' Then Adam says, 'You know, that makes a lot of sense.' And so they eat from the tree and the work begins."

Removing a piece from the board, the man said, "I'd say that makes Eve sound like a smart young lady."

"Sure does," said the boy, peering at what remained. "Amazing how in one version she's blamed for all of suffering, and in another she's full of wisdom."

"Yes," said the man, "but from what we can see in the Scripture, that's not how the story goes."

"That's because there isn't any dialogue recorded between them," said the boy. "But should we assume the first husband and wife never actually spoke to each other? Anyway, I also love how when God says, 'Have you eaten from the tree of which I commanded you not to eat,' everyone assumes He's shouting, with lightning bolts coming out of His eyes, full of vinegar and ready to smite somebody."

"Now here I agree with you," said the man, "but let's hear what you have to say first."

"Well the text doesn't portray anger if you read it plainly," said the boy. "It could be read as a tone of normal conversation, proud even. Like, 'How did you figure out I wanted you to eat from the tree even though I sent you a conflicting message?' And instead of blaming Eve, maybe Adam was giving her credit when he said, 'The woman whom You gave to be with me, she gave me fruit from the tree, and I ate.'"

"Never considered it that way," said the man.

"And maybe what God meant by, 'It's not good that the man should be alone so I'll make him a helper,' was that He knew Adam would never figure it out on his own."

"Mhm," said the man, patiently waiting with his hands folded before him.

"Maybe the punishments weren't punishments at all, but more like, 'Hey, just understand, if you choose to go down to the lower world, there will be things like pain in childbirth and suffering when tilling the soil for food. It ain't like up here where you're lounging around picking fruit off trees in paradise.'"

"It certainly paints a different image than the conventional understanding," said the man. "I believe it's your move."

"I know, I know," said the boy, scanning the board. "But apparently the English idea of original 'sin' is a translation of the Hebrew word 'het,' which doesn't mean what we think it means. This rabbi said it's something like 'a step down,' meaning they *chose* to step down into the lower world."

"So why did God tell them not to eat the fruit in this version," said the man, "if that's what He really wanted?"

"Before we get to that, what were you gonna say when you agreed with me?"

"Well, I never saw God's reaction as anger either," said the man, "more like heartbreak."

"How so?"

"Well, God had planned for His children to live with Him in paradise in the presence of His love, and instead they chose to disobey. Instead of just ignorance and bliss, they could now see evil, recognize their defiance, and so they became ashamed. God is upset that His children now have to live this way. But rather than casting them out of paradise as an act of punishment, I saw His sending them away as an act of mercy, for if they also ate from the tree of life, then they would be immortal in a state of shame in the presence of God. In other words," said the man, "they would have turned their paradise into Hell. To cut them off from the garden, to have the cherubim guard the tree of life, to spare them from this self-created eternity by acting on free will, God allows them to exist in a relationship with Him in a different manner. Only the serpent gets 'cursed,'" said the man. "Adam and Eve are merely taught lessons about the consequence of disobeying God, and how love requires sacrifice."

"What do you mean by that?"

"Well, Eve's sacrifice becomes pain in childbirth, to bring forth the children she'll love. And Adam will toil in sweat through thorns and thistles, to provide for the family he'll love. And God makes them garments out of skins, sacrificing His beloved animals in order to clothe the children He loves."

"I see what you're saying," said the boy.

"But now that Adam and Eve have the knowledge of both good and evil, there's no return to an unconscious paradise.

There's a lot of work on the horizon to prepare for an unpredictable future. They recognize their vulnerability, as you pointed out, as well as their mortality, as well as the vulnerability and mortality of their children for whom they'll need to care for. So a lot of responsibility is placed on their shoulders when it comes to God's command to 'be fruitful and multiply, to fill the earth and subdue it.' The present must now be sacrificed to work for security in the future."

"Right," said the boy. "Self-awareness separates us from the animals, but there's a price to pay for waking up."

"Precisely," said the man. "The end of ignorant bliss in blindly living in the present paradise and the beginning of history as we know it."

"Mmm," said the boy with a nod. "But why was God heartbroken then? If He wanted us to go forth and multiply, wouldn't it be good to have the foresight to see what makes us vulnerable?"

"I think the heartbreak comes from the knowledge of evil," said the man.

"Go on."

"Well, in recognizing what makes you vulnerable, you can also recognize what makes *others* vulnerable."

"Okay…"

"Well, now that we've listened to that little devil whispering in our ear once, we're apt to do it again, and therefore exists the possibility of exploiting the vulnerabilities of others. God was upset because the human propensity for evil was born in that moment, and now He's sent it off into the world He's just created."

"Ohhh," said the boy. "That's good stuff right there."

"So why did God tell them not to eat the fruit in your version?" said the man.

"Well, it's not *my* version," said the boy. "I try to keep my opinion out of it."

"Fair enough," said the man. "Same question though."

"I think it was more like, 'Look, you really don't *want* to eat from that tree, because when you do, you'll step down into a world of pain and have to see both good *and* evil as I do. Up here it's all nice and rosy, but if you're willing, I could really use your help down there. I just want you to choose for yourselves.'"

"I see," said the old man, offering an open palm toward the board.

"It was more of a, 'I don't want you to suffer, and you probably don't want to suffer, but I could use your help if you're willing to suffer.'" The boy jumped his knight to a spot near the man's king, and the man's eyebrows perked up. "We can even weave your view in there so when they make their choice, God gives them clothing as gratitude. Or rather, they sacrifice the immediate pleasures of paradise and agree to suffer for the greater good of mankind, so their sacrifice is rewarded."

"I'm not sure that's exactly how it goes," said the man, still examining the boy's move, "but at least it sounds nice."

"Who knows?" said the boy. "What version are you reading from anyway?"

"New King James," said the man.

"Have you tried another one?"

"Not really. My wife gave me this one years ago, so there's sentimental value."

"You might be surprised at what different translations have to offer," said the boy.

"I'd like to think I'm more attached to the book itself and less to the minor tweaks of language inside," said the man.

"You say they're minor, yet it's the only version you've tried in all these years. I'll bring another translation for you next time."

"That's fine," said the man. "I can't imagine they're so different it changes the storyline."

"I don't know," said the boy. "I've heard the English versions described as 'problematic' at times. I've heard the ancient authors' works were translated by a couple of English snobs saying, 'I don't particularly care for this, so I'm gonna add that instead.'"

"What are some examples?" said the man.

"Here's one you won't like," said the boy, pressing himself up to peer into the pages. "Can you go back to the part about cursing the snake?"

"Sure," said the man, turning the book so they could both see the page. "What are you looking for?"

"Right there," said the boy, pointing to the verse.

And I will put enmity
Between you and the woman,
And between your seed and her Seed.
He shall bruise your head,
And you shall bruise His heel.[7]

"You see where the *S* in 'Seed' and the *H* in 'His' are capitalized?"

"Mhm."

"Why do you think that is?"

"Why, that's a nod to Christ coming down the line," said the man.

"Right, but Jesus wouldn't exist for another couple thousand years after that was written."

"And what's your point?"

"Oh nothing," said the boy, lowering himself down again. "I just think it's interesting they don't appear with translators who can read ancient Hebrew, that's all."

The old man stayed silent, but his jaw clenched visibly.

"Look, I think it's a clever little nod by believers that Christ was the Messiah," said the boy, "but on the topic of honest translations, you have to admit that's a big creative liberty."

"Well," said the man, a bit stiff in his ways, "New King James *is* the translation by those who believe Christ was the Messiah."

"Look, I'm not saying the interpretation is *wrong*," said the boy. "Like I said, I try to keep opinion out of it. But as far as translations go, I thought it was interesting to point out. That's all."

"Mhm," said the man, his demeanor melting slowly.

"Look, I'll bring the other book tomorrow so we can read side-by-side," said the boy. "But another thing that stuck out was replacing the word 'semen' with things like 'seed' or 'offspring,' so we don't burn the eyes of prudes or whatever."

"I see," said the man, shifting uncomfortably.

"I just don't understand who has the audacity to take what is supposed to be the Word of God and say, 'Ya know, I don't really care for God's choice here. I think I'll supersede the Almighty and write my own.' Who does that, ya know? If the word means semen and we have a word for semen, then stick to semen!" said the boy, playfully pounding a fist on the table. "No pun intended."

"That's crude," said the man.

"See what I mean about the prudes?"

The old man exhaled a forced laugh through his nose as he moved a piece on the board.

"*Finally*," said the boy. "Take long enough?"

"Yeah, yeah," said the man. "Your turn."

The boy stood up to heave his backpack over his shoulder, and the old man stared at him, confused. "That was already checkmate," said the boy. "I just wanted to school you a little longer." The man shot a glance down at the board again as the boy said, "I've gotta eat something before I get some work done. See you tomorrow?"

Without looking up, searching for a mistake, the man said, "I'll be here," but the boy was already gone.

GENESIS 4-5

CAIN & ABEL

Let us go out to the field.
—Cain

"Listen to the difference," said the boy. "Read that line from your book and I'll read it from this guy who knows ancient Hebrew."[8]

So the man read aloud:

Then the Lord said to Cain, "Why are you furious? And why do you look despondent? If you do what is right, won't you be accepted? But if you do not do what is right, sin is crouching at the door. Its desire is for you, but you must rule over it."[9]

Then the boy read aloud:

"Why are you incensed, and why is your face fallen? For whether you offer well, or whether you do not, at the tent flap sin crouches and for you is its longing, but you will rule over it."

"They're a bit different," said the man, "but the meaning isn't exactly lost."

"I'm not saying this particular example is appalling," said the boy, "and I get that it's modernized because we no longer live in tents or whatever, but who's to say what liberties should be taken where when doing an honest translation? It's a slippery slope, ya know?"

"I see what you're saying," said the man.

"Let's keep reading from yours though," said the boy. "I'll follow along in this one and speak up if anything stands out."

"Alright then," said the man, looking down again. "Where were we?" He began skimming aloud to find where they left off. "Adam knows Eve and bears Cain, then his brother Abel... Cain offers the fruit of the ground, Abel the first of his flock... The Lord respects Abel's offering but not Cain's... Ah. Here we are," said the man:

> Now Cain talked with Abel his brother, and it came to pass, when they were in the fiel—

"Lemme stop you right there because it leaves out a line that I have here. Listen to this," said the boy:

> And Cain said to Abel his brother, "Let us go out to the field." And when they were in the field, Cain rose against Abel his brother and killed him.[10]

The boy looked up at the man. "Now why would they leave that out? Is the result any different? No, Abel still dies. But why take out the part where Cain invites him into the field to make it sound otherwise?"

"I really don't know," said the man. "But as you mentioned, the result is the same."

"Like I said, nothing major, but we're only a few pages into the book and they're already taking stuff out just because they feel like it. Makes you wonder how much of that there is by the time we get to page five hundred, or page one thousand."

"I guess we'll see. Although at this rate," the man laughed, "I'm not sure we'll get to the end before *I* die."

The boy smiled as he reached for his first move.

The man watched him advance a pawn before turning his eyes back to the pages:

Then the Lord said to Cain, "Where is Abel your brother?"

He said, "I do not know. Am I my brother's keeper?"

And He said, "What have you done? The voice of your brother's blood cries out to Me from the ground."[11]

"I just wanna point out how manipulative God was again," said the boy.

"What do you mean?"

"What do you mean, 'What do you mean?' I mean what did Cain do wrong?"

The man raised an eyebrow. "You don't think killing your brother is wrong?"

"No, not that," said the boy. "Before that. They both made an offering and God played favorites. Why, because He wasn't in the mood for fruit that day? What if Cain brought Him some mint jelly to go with that lamb instead of some berries or whatever? Would God have been pleased then?"

"You have quite the imagination," said the man. "You know, some have guessed that while Abel brought the best of his flock, Cain didn't offer the best of his crops, but I don't see evidence there. And someone once told me the reason for God's partiality was based on the line, 'Now Abel was a keeper of sheep, but Cain was a tiller of land.' He said there was a heavy emphasis on the 'but,' meaning God preferred man to be nomadic herders, multiplying to subdue the earth rather than stay in one place to farm."

"But wasn't Cain following in his father's footsteps," said the boy, "based on the way God told Adam to till and eat from the soil?"

"Precisely," said the man. "I don't agree with that notion either. I think Adam likely pursued both occupations after God showed him how to make clothing from skins. And so because each of his sons chose a noble occupation in the eyes of the Lord, I see it as proof it wasn't *what* they offered that pleased or displeased the Lord, but *how* they made their offering. My guess is that while Abel made his offering from the depths of his heart to honor the Lord, Cain offered merely to remain in God's good graces. Some go as far as to say that Cain was inherently evil and lived a wicked lif—"

"Where are you getting *that* from?" said the boy.

"Well, because he goes on to kill his brother."

"Yeah, but point to where it shows any sign of Cain being wicked *before* God plays favorites. He makes an offering of his profession just like Abel, so if that's the direction you wanna go, it's something of a chicken-or-egg scenario. I'd say it's a leap to assume Cain was evil beforehand when there's no evidence for it. Meanwhile we *do* have evidence for God's actions causing a *re*action in Cain. Who's to say if God didn't favor Cain that day, then Abel wouldn't have done the same?"

"We'll never know for sure," said the man.

"I can't help but to sympathize with Cain on this one," said the boy. "Think about it. You're one of four people on the earth back then. God obviously loves your parents because He created them, but He rejects you in favor of your younger brother for seemingly no good reason. What's up with that? Wouldn't you be upset?"

"I suppose I would," said the man.

"Of course you would!" said the boy. "And then He comes at him with the old asking-questions-to-which-I-already-know-the-answers routine? Jerk move right there."

"I take it you have a younger brother?"

"And how would Cain even know what it means to kill someone? No one's seen death at this point, so how can God expect him to know the consequence of hitting someone over the head with a rock or whatever? Maybe Cain didn't mean to take it that far, but God didn't exactly offer a warning."

The man raised another eyebrow. "Did you hit your brother with a rock?"

"Or maybe God offered a warning off-screen that the narrator didn't mention. Maybe God says, 'Thou shall not hit someone over the head with a rock, for if you do they'll surely die.' And Cain rolls his eyes and thinks, *Suuure, God. The old 'surely die' trick again, just like you played on our mother.* You know what I'm sayin'?"

The old man smiled. "Let's suppose God was being as unfair as you're implying. Perhaps their offerings are equal in the sense that each man brings the best of his trade. But maybe God recognizes an underlying jealousy in Cain, so He creates a situation that will probe at his character. Cain is jealous because he thinks God favored his brother, but perhaps the offerings were never about a lamb or fruit of the ground at all, but rather a test for Cain to pass."

The boy's fire seemed to melt as the idea sunk in.

"The questions He asked are, 'Why are you furious? And why do you look despondent? If you do what is right, won't you be accepted?' He's asking Cain to do the right thing, and if he doesn't, He warns him that evil will surface and there may be consequences. God doesn't immediately reject Cain. Just like He asks Adam why he hid to give him a chance to repent, God asks Cain why he's angry so he can recognize his jealousy and amend it."

"Yeah, well, maybe," said the boy, calmer now. "Where did this idea of offering a sacrificial lamb come from anyway? Seems so barbaric."

"Well that's not as primitive as you make it out to seem," said the man. "In many ways, it's far more sophisticated than the mindset we have today."

"How so?"

"Well, let's consider it in the context we unpacked with Adam and Eve. We've become conscious of our vulnerability, cast from paradise, and now we have to sacrifice the present to work to ensure our preparedness for the future. The idea of sacrificing something valuable in order to remain in God's good graces is by no means an unsophisticated notion. Because what is the alternative to ensure preservation? Murder and theft perhaps, or something else along the evil path. Unless you would've had a better idea, this may have been one of the greatest ideas humans ever came up with."

"I see what you're saying," said the boy. "I guess I wasn't thinking about it in the context of the times."

"Today you order pizza to your door and never think twice. You probably don't offer any kind of thanks to whoever delivered it, or who made it, or who farmed and raised the ingredients you topped it with. I'll guess you don't even pray before your meals either, do you?"

"No," said the boy. "There's truth in all of that."

"When have you offered a degree of thanks even close to the slaughter of an animal? My guess is never."

"Also true," said the boy.

"Have you ever killed an animal by your own hand to put food on the table?"

"No," said the boy, "I haven't."

"Well, son, not only are we on different pages, but we're not even in the same book."

"I take it you have?"

"I grew up on a farm," said the man. "My father had me slaughtering pigs by the time I was eight years old."

"Wow," said the boy. "*That's* intense."

"It's a different level of connectivity with your food and the relationship with the world around you."

"I see your point," said the boy. "And I guess there must be something to the idea if it's cropped up in numerous cultures around the world."

"Making sacrifices is part of the human experience," said the man. "You've just been raised in a time where it appears ir-relevant."

The boy stared into the old man's eyes, nodding in silence. To break the tension, he pointed to the man's book and said, "So what does God say to Cain next?"

The old man looked down at the page to find his place again and read:

"So now you are cursed from the earth, which has opened its mouth to receive your brother's blood from your hand. When you till the ground, it shall no longer yield its strength to you. A fugitive and a vagabond you shall be."[12]

"Here it says, 'A *restless wanderer* shall you be,'" said the boy. "Which, again, is a subtle difference, but a fugitive is someone who escaped from prison or whatever and is on the run. Cain wasn't on the run from some Johnny Law that didn't exist back then. He was exiled, which is different."

"I can agree with that," said the man.

"Anyway, keep going."

So the man read on:

And Cain said to the Lord, "My punishment is greater than I can bear! Surely You have driven me out this day from the face of the ground. I shall be hidden from Your face, I shall be a fugitive and a vagabond on the earth, and it will happen that anyone who finds me will kill me."[13]

"Who are they talking about?" said the boy. "Cain is the only human other than his parents at this point."

"I guess that's a detail the Scripture leaves out," said the man.

"Detail," said the boy. "Hole," he added, balancing the words with his hands like a scale. "Anywa—"

"Well hold on," said the man. "Let's not just brush over that criticism you made."

"I didn't really mean anything by it," said the boy.

"But you didn't hesitate to point it out either," said the man. "I hear remarks like this and I wonder, is that really the best you can come up with to attack a literary masterpiece? And moreover, does it really matter? Take the 'Little Red Riding Hood' example you brought up yesterday. One could easily say, 'Well that's silly. Wolves don't talk.'"

"Hmm," said the boy. "I see what you're saying."

"Critics of the Bible get so caught up in the details that they try to discount the whole Scripture as nonsense, but they're missing the bigger picture. No, wolves don't talk, but it doesn't mean a lesson on moving through life with caution can't be derived from the story either. And perhaps there's an inconsistency here or there in the biblical texts, but it doesn't diminish the lesson from a tale of two men that ends in the death of the best one of them, a story that's played out in history time and time again because we never learn."

"Very true," said the boy.

"These stories are so compact that picking out trivial details defeats the purpose. 'Who are these other people?' is a simple-minded question that distracts from how far jealousy can push a man to kill not only his brother, but the best part of himself as well, not to mention his relationship with God moving forward."

"Alright, alright," said the boy. "I was being simple-minded and take back what I said. Can *we* move forward?"

"We sure can," said the man. "I'll let you do the honors."

So the boy read from his text this time:

And the Lord set a mark upon Cain so that whoever found him would not slay him.[14]

The boy looked up from his book and said, "Do you think that's to spare him from a rough encounter, or make his punishment worse by denying him from being put out of his misery?"

"I think those are one in the same," said the man. "In spite of the fact that God is displeased, He still reveals a core dimension of His nature, which is mercy. But to take it a step further, we glossed over God's line, 'When you till the ground, it shall no longer yield its strength to you.' This is important because God robs Cain of his purpose in life as a farmer. And now as a man without a purpose, he's been outcast as an aimless wanderer, as your book says. Painful in its own right, but by marking him, God extends the longevity of his purposeless existence."

"Ahh," said the boy, "I missed that part."

"The mark also reminds others that evil should not be repaid by evil," said the man. "Those who came across Cain may have wanted revenge for having gone against God's will, for causing the pain that he caused, for killing a valuable member of society as a shepherd, which, in those times, was an important and difficult task. But knowing they'd receive God's vengeance sevenfold would have caused anyone to think twice about whether or not it was worth it. It would have made them realize that killing Cain would only cause more suffering, not to mention punishment for themselves."

"Riiight," said the boy. "I overlooked that as well."

"Easy to do with these stories," said the man. "Brief as they are, there's a lot to absorb."

The boy nodded and read on:

And Cain went out from the Lord's presence and dwelled in the land of Nod east of Eden. And Cain knew his wife and she conceived and bore Enoch.[15]

The boy began paraphrasing and said, "Then Enoch has a son who has a son who has a son who has a son named Lamech, who takes two wives and knocks 'em both up. I'm just breezing over this because I wanna hear you read Lamech's speech here."

"Very well," said the man:

"Adah and Zillah, hear my voice. Wives of Lamech, pay attention to my words. For I killed a man for wounding me, a young man for striking me. If Cain is to be avenged seven times over, then for Lamech it will be seventy-seven times!"[16]

"He's bragging about killing a boy and taunting God with a higher bounty, right?" said the boy.

"That's what I gathered, yes."

"Just making sure. So then we jump back to Adam, who knocks up Eve again, and she pops out Seth as a replacement for Abel." The old man smiled and shook his head. "Then Seth wastes no time having a son himself, and then in my version there's the line that says, 'It was then that the name of the Lord was first invoked,' which I was hoping you could clarify."

"Here it's, 'Then men began to call on the name of the Lord.' And I've heard this one debated," said the man, "but I've always read into it as a line to emphasize the lineage of Cain versus Seth. Cain's line seems to be deviating from the path, becoming violent and taking up polygamy. So when Adam and Eve start a new line by giving birth to Seth, there becomes a more righteous and faithful line that God favors, as we'll see unfold in the coming story."

"Ah, okay," said the boy. "I guess that makes sense."

"At least that's my opinion," said the man.

"Next they list Adam's genealogy and begin by mentioning God created man in His likeness. Then it says Adam lived nine hundred and thirty years before he had Seth in his own likeness. We'll put the lifespans of these early people aside, but you think these parallel 'in likeness' lines are to further differentiate Seth's line from Cain's?"

"I do," said the man.

"I will say that Adam's time was a pretty good run," said the boy, "but a tad anti-climactic when all we hear is 'and he died.'"

"Again, I think it's one of those details left out for brevity's sake," said the man. "He played his role in the story and we've learned from him all we can."

"With the time span these people lived back then, it makes you wonder if Adam didn't sneak a teensy piece of that tree of life on his way out the door." The old man smiled as the boy said, "Poor Eve though. Mother of all living things and her death isn't even mentioned."

"I'll admit the biblical stories leave something to be desired regarding women at times," said the man, "but this is all we have."

"Well," said the boy, letting out a big sigh, "she bore sons, so at least she served a purpose." The old man rolled his eyes. "Speaking of Eve," said the boy, "the rest of this chapter lists out their line and how many hundreds of years they all lived. Is there any significance to this other than the fact we land on Noah, who 'will console us for the pain of our hands' work from the soil which the Lord cursed'?"

"It gives us a timeline of how many years passed before the flood," said the man. "But once we get to Noa—"

"Actually, can we save that for tomorrow?" said the boy. "I've gotta get going."

The old man pointed at the board and said, "But I haven't even taken my first move."

"I know, I know, but I've got some kind of family dinner thingy I'm supposed to go to and I still need a shower."

"Alright," said the old man, "I'll see you tomorrow then."

The boy folded his book shut and stuffed it in his pack. Then he stood up, giving the old man a salute, and wandered off down the path.

NOAH & THE
TOWER OF BABEL

The sons of God came in to the daughters of men
and they bore children to them.
—Genesis 6:4

"So who were the 'sons of God' then?"

"What do you mean?"

"Well you just made a clear distinction that when men began to multiply, the 'sons of God' saw the 'daughters of men' and took wives of their choosing. I want to hear what you think because I've got a pretty good idea."

"Let's hear your idea first," said the man.

"Well, God said He didn't want Adam eating from the tree so man doesn't become like one of '*Us*.' Seems like there's an implication of god*s*, plural, like in ancient Greek mythology."

The old man chuckled. "I think that's a bit of a stretch."

"Is it though? A lot of cultures back then believed in more than one god. Who's to say the influence of Egypt didn't rub off on their neighbors around the time this was written?"

"Well I don't think—"

"There's a clear distinction that these were *sons* of *God*, so who's to say there wasn't some crossbreeding going on, like with Achilles? Your passage just said there were giants on the earth in the days when the sons of God came in to the daughters of men and bore them children. It even called them 'mighty men' and 'men of renown.' There's clearly something strange going on, so why couldn't they be demi-gods, like Hercules?" The boy flexed a skinny pair of arms and the man smiled.

"I don't believe these are literal giants we're speaking of here. In fact, when I looked into it, the King James translations were the only versions where the word 'giants' appears. All the rest use the term 'Nephilim,' which I've also seen translated from Hebrew into 'fallen ones' or even 'those causing others to fall.' Now, to your point of numerous divine beings, I have heard some argue the 'sons of God' refer to angels that came down from the heavens to have relations with mortal women, resulting in these supernatural beings, but it seems farfetched that the first mention of God's holy angels would be spoken of in contempt the way this verse unfolds. Not to mention there's no reference to angels getting married anywhere else in the Bible that I'm aware of, nor any reference to spiritual beings procreating with mortal beings, so why would this single, cryptic line be the only instance it's seen? In my eyes these assumptions are as nonsensical as those pagan myths you proposed."

"Yeah!" said the boy. Then he spat on the ground and said, "*Pagans.*"

The man watched the boy smirk at him, but he chose not to say anything. "Besides, God goes on to punish *men* for their actions, not angels, so one would assume the consequence would be brought on by men's actions, not angels. Which leaves only one perfectly reasonable explanation."

"Oh?" said the boy. "What's that?"

"Well our first clue, I think, goes back to Adam and Eve. When she gives birth to Cain, he's referred to as a man, but when she gives birth to Seth, he's referred to as a son. My understanding is that 'sons of God' refers to Seth's line, who up until now have been calling on the name of the Lord, and 'daughters of men' refers to Cain's line, who have gone astray from God's righteous path. So when humans begin to multiply and the sons of Seth see the daughters of Cain were beautiful, their lines begin to mingle with marriage based on promiscuity instead of spiritual character."

"Ohhh," said the boy. "Well that certainly brings things down to earth again."

"While it sounds flashy when celestial beings come down to claim terrestrial wives, especially when they've yet to be introduced in the text at all, there's no moral lesson we can derive from the story that way. I think a more grounded explanation allows us to heed a warning about choosing a spouse who's aligned with God, or else we become impressionable to ungodly ways. Then we bring Nephilim to earth, meaning children who have fallen off God's path."

"But why were they 'mighty men' and 'men of renown'?"

"Many throughout history are known not for their good, but for their sins," said the man.

"I suppose we could see those 'giants' as men who were too big for their britches," said the boy. "Then the text would read as a cocky narrative. Like, 'Here, here! We've taken the most beautiful women and now we see ourselves as mighty men! You may henceforth refer to us as men of renown!'"

"Perhaps it's something like that," said the man, "sure. But I think this is why the Lord says, 'My Spirit shall not strive with man forever, for he is indeed flesh, yet his days shall be one hundred and twenty years.' The line appears in the middle of a paragraph describing man's deviation from His path and the result, so to me it makes sense God would limit his lifespan from many centuries down to one, given the propensity for sin taking place on the earth at the time."

"Eh. I still kinda like the idea of God drowning a bunch of chumps like Achilles."

"Whoever the Nephilim were," said the man, "the Scripture doesn't say much about them after the flood, so I'm not sure it's worth our breath to discuss them any further."

41

"Alright," said the boy, offering his palm toward the Bible, "let's move past it then."

With a nod the man read on:

When the Lord saw that human wickedness was widespread on the earth, and that every inclination of the human mind was nothing but evil all the time, the Lord regretted that he had made man on the earth, and he was deeply grieved.[17]

"Well this certainly plays into your theory of God being heartbroken."

The old man agreed before reading further:

So the Lord said, "I will destroy man whom I have created from the face of the earth, both man and beast, creeping thing and birds of the air, for I am sorry that I have made them." But Noah found grace in the eyes of the Lord.[18]

"So here it says Noah was 'blameless in his time' and that he 'walked with God,' which I'm assuming means he was the last man on earth to have followed God's will, and why he's the chosen one, right?"

"He and his family, yes," said the man. "God tells Noah that the earth and all its inhabitants are corrupt and full of violence and that He'll destroy them. Here he instructs Noah to build an ark to His specifications and that He plans to bring floodwaters."

"I love how the Sunday school version of this story portrays a cute little cartoon chugging along with a bunch of smiling lions and hippos. Besides the fact Noah somehow corralled a bunch of bloodthirsty man-killers, this isn't a summer vacation cruise. This is God's wrath being rained down upon the earth destroying everything."

"But how early should you expose children to that kind of death and destruction?" said the man.

"Says the guy who was slaughtering pigs by eight years old. Yet here you are."

"I guess that's true," said the man.

"God's feeling particularly talkative today though. Besides cursing everyone in chapter three, He's barely strung a few words together. All it took was a little intermingling of blood-lines to ruffle His feathers and now He's just yappin' away about destruction, telling Noah to wrangle up enough food for two of everything."

"And Noah was wise to listen," said the man, "because in a week's time God says He'll make it rain for forty days and forty nights."

"And the poor guy was supposed to be six-hundred years old at this point," said the boy. "Makes you wonder how his back was holding up after building a giant ark in a week. It's like, jeez, God, couldn't the poor guy get a little more time at his age?"

The old man laughed. "I think he built the ark and *then* God told him to gather the animals a week before the flood, but my back hurts thinking about it either way."

"Imagine trying to carry a couple *rhinos* over your shoulder," said the boy with a wink.

"Trees for the forest," said the man, and he was about to read on when the boy stopped him.

"Actually, I was doubtful about how realistic the dimensions of the ark would have been for the task, but I found an article where a bunch of physics students found the dimensions the Bible gave for the wood used. They took into consideration the average weight of around seventy-thousand animals and the buoyancy of water, and apparently it adds up."

"Well there," said the man, "you see?"

"Doesn't mean it happened," said the boy. "It just means the narrators had the foresight to imagine a really big boat." The old man raised a finger in the air to object, but the boy cut him off. "Look, I don't want to get into the weeds about the feasibility of how Noah managed to get two kangaroos to swim from Australia to the Middle East and back again after an impossible amount of water recedes to nowhere. We'll never agree on the story as a factual history the way it's described, but I do think there is enough evidence for cataclysmic floods that could have *inspired* this story."

"Alright," said the old man, "I'm listening."

"Well first of all, the story of Noah isn't exactly an original, you know that, right?"

"What do you mean?" said the man.

"Well, there are flood myths from different cultures all around the world. A number of them even share this narrative where a powerful deity comes down to earth to erase all of life, minus a chosen few in a boat. Now, there seems to be evidence for massive floods in different places on earth, but they happened at different times. And many of the other stories reference great floods, but not all of them mention *global* floods. My guess is that we see this shared experience because early humans were bound to settle near water for survival reasons, so they lived in prime flooding landscapes, which is common."

The man stared questioningly but unconvinced.

"The similar stories I mentioned all came from the neighboring regions of India, Greece, and the Middle East, and there's evidence for a giant flood around there a few thousand years before the Biblical stories were written down. The aftermath of a major event like a super volcano or meteor could have melted a lot of the ice buildup there and caused a huge increase in water levels. It's possible the rumors got passed down from generation to generation and used as the inspiration for the story we're reading now."

The man sat quietly listening with his arms crossed.

"If we're trying to recount this story as historical," said the boy, "Noah's 'earth' was only as far as the eye could see when man still traveled on foot. Back when the earth was flat and the center of the universe and all, whoever was around couldn't just pull out their GPS and livestream the earth turning blue from a satellite. But the earth from *their* point of view could have been covered in water as far as the eye could see, inspiring a story about an unbelievable event and then justified as an act of God. At least that would make sense to apply a moral lesson for future generations not to make Him angry. But I think we also have to take into consideration the human tendency for embellishing stories told around a campfire."

"Mhm," said the man, unwavering in his stance.

"We can also look at the flood from another point of view," said the boy.

"How so?" said the man.

"Well, someone can imagine a metaphorical flood of chaos on the horizon," said the boy, "and prepare for it, maybe even prevent it from happening. But if they can't, at least they can ride it out. Noah could see that things weren't going well, and maybe God even gave him a heads-up because Noah walked with God in the sense that he's tuned into some kind of intuition from the great beyond, because he's not distracted by the human tendency toward evil or whatever. So he had the foresight to see a little further into the future than most people and he prepared for it. And because he prepared, things actually went pretty well for Noah, considering the circumstance, whereas others who were distracted and unprepared suffered and perished."

"But this *was* a real event Noah prepared for," said the man.

"Sure, sure," said the boy. "I won't try to convince you, I just thought I'd throw it out there. All I'm saying is that we can look beyond the literal account to take away a warning to apply to modern-day life as well."

"I see what you're getting at," said the man.

"Here's a question for you," said the boy. "In order to be a Christian, do you *have* to accept everything in the Bible as fact? Like say I bought into everything else, but I didn't think the flood was feasible. Would I still burn in Hell?"

"There's something called 'biblical inerrancy,'" said the man, "where the Holy Scripture is the Word of God and therefore carries the full authority of God. This means every statement in the Bible calls for acceptance, every doctrine requires agreement."

"Jeez, that's strict," said the boy. "But who said that, you know? You heard it from some guy who heard it from some guy who heard it from some guy going back a thousand years. This could be a fear-driven command tagged on at any point in a game of telephone by Pastor Joe Schmo in response to a little Johnny who started thinking for himself, probably when people began to read instead of relying on a select few to preach at us."

"I imagine it came at the beginning," said the man, "and I never dared question it."

"That's my pet peeve about organized religion right there though. We have stories that are ripe for interpretation, but the influencers in power told us if you don't believe them you'll burn. Meanwhile we don't even know who wrote them or what their original meanings were. I imagine there are some people out there that call themselves Christians who have trouble believing *everything*, you know? I mean how do you get a couple *billion* people on the same page when it comes to nearly a million words of text?"

"I suppose that's why there are more than forty-five-thousand Christian denominations across the globe," said the man.

"*Whaaat?*" said the boy. "That's insane! How do you think Jesus would feel about that today?"

With a slight groan, the old man said, "I don't care to speculate."

"Where do you draw the line with this stuff though?" said the boy. "What if Bob follows everything the Good Book says but has trouble believing in the flood? Then you have Sally, a flood believer who sins every other day but repents on Sunday. Is Sally allowed into Heaven just because she's convinced of the flood, but Bob is left out because he had a degree in geology even though he lived a more righteous life?"

"That's between Bob or Sally and God when they get to the heavenly gates," said the man.

"Alright, well, we'll never agree on the flood being true, but let's see what else we can take away."

"Fair enough," said the man, running his finger down the text and paraphrasing. "Let's see here. Noah and his family were on the ark… It rained for forty days… The earth floods and everything was destroyed… Then the waters prevailed for one hundred and fifty days."

"And the waters took forever to recede," said the boy, skimming his own text, "but when they did, Noah built an altar, burnt something that smelled good, and pleased the Lord. So the Lord promised never to curse the ground or flood everything again, which is a sweet relief."

"Actually," said the man, "it's worth noting that this is something God promises 'in His heart,' meaning to Himself, not out loud. His first words to Noah and his sons after the flood are, 'Be fruitful and multiply.'"

"Right. Then He turns to setting a bunch of rules to follow for how the post-flood life should be. Like we're allowed to eat animals now, right?"

"Yes. It's also worth noting that our relationship with animals has changed," said the man. "Where in Eden it was one of dominion, now it's adversarial, based on fear and dread."

"Perhaps another reference to how we've fallen out of the order that was paradise and now live in something closer to chaos," said the boy.

"It's also made clear 'you shall not eat flesh with its life, that is, its blood.' This is the first time blood is mentioned as something to be respected, tied to life, and something we'll see build upon itself as the books unfold."

"Right, then He pivots to the new rules laid out for shedding the blood of other humans," said the boy.

"That's right. Before the flood, God seemed more forgiving with Cain, letting him live on and have children. But here He requires a reckoning, saying anyone who takes another man's life shall pay with his own bloodshed."

"So God puts the responsibility of punishment in man's hands this time?"

"Something like that," said the man.

"Then it looks like God signed the contract with a rainbow."

The old man laughed. "Yes, God tells Noah, 'The rainbow shall be in the cloud, and I will look on it to remember the everlasting covenant between God and every living creature of all flesh that is on the earth.'"

"That's pretty slick."

"Indeed," said the man. "Shall we keep going, or do you have another dinner?"

"I've got a little while longer," said the boy, "although I think it's too late to start a game."

"That's alright," said the man, "I can play Chess anytime. It's not often enough I get to enjoy these conversations."

"Very true," said the boy, peering down at his text again. "Alright, well maybe you can explain this next part to me then, because I never got it. Noah's sons Shem and Ham and Japheth and their wives come out of the boat and go on to populate the earth. I'll overlook the jokes about cousin lovin' and get straight to the confusing part," said the boy, glancing quickly up at the man with a smirk. The man stared blankly back, so the boy went on. "So Noah plants the first vineyard and gets drunk and then 'exposed himself within his tent.' This means he passed out naked right?"

"Mhm," said the man, "that's my understanding."

"Okay, but here's the confusing part:

> Ham, the father of Canaan, saw the nakedness of his father, and told his two brothers outside. But Shem and Japheth took a garment and laid it on both their shoulders and walked backward and covered the nakedness of their father, and their faces were turned away, so that they did not see their father's nakedness.
>
> When Noah awoke from his wine, he knew what his youngest son had done to him. So he said, "Cursed be Canaan, a servant of servants He shall be to his brothers."[19]

The boy looked up at the man and said, "What just happened there?"

"Well," said the old man, shifting uncomfortably, "there are a few interpretations of those lines. The more innocent one is that Ham walked in on his father passed out drunk and nude. In those times, it was shameful to see someone in that condition. I suppose this is a warning early on in the Bible about the consequence of drinking alcohol, but Ham took it a step further by gossiping about it to his brothers."

"Oh," said the boy. "That doesn't seem like such a big deal to get cursed over though."

"Maybe not today," said the old man, "but Shem and Japheth's actions reveal how seriously their culture took the issue of seeing another naked. They found a way to cover Noah with creativity and care, without looking at him and honoring their father in that way."

"Gotcha."

"Also, consider Noah is not only the sole father of the new world in the manner in which you're thinking now, not to mention the man who just saved humanity through the flood, but he also represents the *spirit* of the father in some sense. By humiliating his father when he's most vulnerable for making humanity's first mistake in getting drunk, Ham loses respect for the spirit of the father. And without the spirit of the father in your life, well, you can become lost. You understand what I mean?"

"I think so," said the boy. "Like when my parents split up I kinda lost the sense of having a real family dynamic, so I lost the spirit of the family?"

"I'm sorry to hear that," said the man, "but, yes, I imagine that's a fair comparison."

"What are the less innocent interpretations?"

"Well," said the old man, shifting uncomfortably again, "you see, there are some who believe that 'seeing their father's nakedness' is an idiomatic expression for, well, laying with their father's, um... wife."

"He fucked his mom?" said the boy. "Man, I was just kidding about the inbreeding, but that's another level!"

"Well," said the man, straightening his posture and putting his hands in his lap, "in this context it wasn't so much an act of lust as it was one of domination, humiliating or emasculating his father in that way."

"Wait, but then why does it say Noah 'knew what his youngest son had done *to him*'? Doesn't that mean he—"

"*You know*," said the old man, pressing his hands onto the table and propping himself up to leave, "I think that's enough for today."

"No, no, wait," said the boy. "Let's just skip to the Tower of Babel so we can start on Abram next time. One more chapter and we'll call it a day." The man stood frozen, halfway between sitting and standing. "Come on," said the boy. "One more. We can't end on *that* note."

The man eased back down and said, "Alright. One more. Only because I love how much is packed into so few words here."

"Thank you," said the boy.

"But let's try to keep the language to a minimum," said the old man. "I'm too old for that shit."

They both laughed as the boy skimmed through to the Tower of Babel. "Alright, so Noah's sons multiply and they journey from the east to settle in a land called Shinar. Here, why don't you read since you love this one."

"I'd love to," said the man:

Then they said to one another, "Come, let us make bricks and bake them thoroughly." They had brick for stone, and they had tar for mortar. And they said, "Come, let us build ourselves a city, and a tower whose top is in the heavens. Let us make a name for ourselves, lest we be scattered abroad over the face of the whole earth."[20]

The man paused and looked up, but the boy said, "Keep going. I like the way what God says parallels what man does."

So the man read on:

Then the Lord came down to look over the city and the tower that the humans were building. The Lord said, "If they have begun to do this as one people all having the same language, then nothing they plan to do will be impossible for them. Come, let's go down there and confuse their language so that they will not understand one another's speech." So from there the Lord scattered them throughout the earth, and they stopped building the city.[21]

"'Therefore it is called Babel,'" read the boy, "'for there the Lord made the language of all the earth babble. And from there the Lord scattered them over all the earth.' Love that. Man says, 'Come, let us bake bricks,' God says, 'Come, let Us go down.' Man is concerned with being scattered, God scatters them."

"Nice parallels indeed," said the man. "Man has become so ambitious that he thinks he no longer needs God to ascend to Heaven."

"Oh really?" said the boy. "Is that your take?"

"It says it right there," said the man, pointing at the verse.

"Well it says 'top in the heavens,' but I figured this was an exaggeration for celebrating high towers. You think man was actually trying to break its way back into the garden?"

54

"Why else would God have to put a stop to the ambition? He sees that man is getting along and working in harmony, which is good, but the project they choose to work on is bad. They want to break the heaven-and-earth divide, perhaps to ascend and communicate with God directly, or even elevate themselves above Him. But the heavens were not meant for man unless God declared it, so man tried to take matters into their own hands."

"I don't know where you're getting that from though," said the boy. "All it says is man wanted to make a name for himself, nothing about ambitions to communicate with God or escape the earth. As far as we know, everyone who once spoke to God or knew about Eden is dead. For all we know the rumor of Heaven may have been lost years ago. Seems like you're filling in blanks that aren't there."

"I suppose I'm reading between the lines," said the man. "But man supposes happiness can be found in autonomy, so he builds a city where he can create his own laws instead of follow God's. In the city, man is powerful, perhaps even evil."

"Yeah, but point to where God says cities and government are evil," said the boy. "So Cain succumbed to evil and went on to build a city. That doesn't make cities evil. What's that phrase about causation and correlation? If anything, God gives them rules on *how* to govern themselves, like in the case of murder after the flood."

"Well how do you interpret the story then?"

"I thought man was trying to build a permanent landmark so they would always know where home base was, so they didn't get scattered. But this defies God's command to go forth and multiply and subdue the earth or whatever. That's what He keeps telling them anyway. But they seem resistant to it. They seem to wanna stay together in one place and accomplish great things in architecture."

"Hmm," said the man, stroking his beard. "I guess your interpretation is the one bringing things down to earth this time."

"I'm not saying you're wrong," said the boy, "it just seems like you're seeing things that aren't there. I think if God was afraid they'd build some kind of ladder where they could just come and go from Heaven whenever they pleased, He would have told them not to."

"Ahh, but inevitably there would have been some who defied Him," said the man, "which would leave God no choice but to use force and aggression to teach a lesson again, something He promised not to do. I think confusing the languages was a benign way of dissuading them from finishing the tower."

"I have to wonder if there's a more rational meaning to this story," said the boy, "tying it back to the event we just witnessed. Civilization was blooming in one area with language and architecture and then all the sudden the flood destroyed most of civilization, and the few survivors scattered in different directions and developed their own cultures and languages that branched off from the original one."

The man paused before he said, "I don't think—"

"Yeah, yeah, yeah, you think it's literal history," said the boy. "I'm just thinking out loud here. Anyway, maybe we sorta figured it out together, or maybe we're both completely off the mark and have no idea what we're talking about."

The man smiled. "Fair enough. What do you say we stop there for today though. This old man's brain is getting tired."

"Alright," said the boy, "sounds good. See you tomorrow?"

"I'll be here," said the man, pressing himself to stand again.

The boy did the same, and with a nod, they went their separate ways.

GENESIS 12-15

ABRAM & SARAI

What is this you have done to me?
—Pharaoh

"So after God scatters men about the earth, Abram emerges from the genealogy of Shem and becomes the focus of our story. And God comes to Abram to tell him this," said the man:

> "Go from your country, your people and your father's household to the land I will show you. I will make you into a great nation, and I will bless you. I will make your name great, and you will be a blessing. I will bless those who bless you, and whoever curses you I will curse, and all peoples on earth will be blessed through you."[22]

"Very trusting, seeing as how God sends him to a mysterious place 'I will show you,'" said the boy.

"Indeed," said the man. "God asks Abram to do a very bold thing by leaving the comfort of home to venture out into an unknown world, therefore testing his faith and obedience. But, as we see, 'Abram departed as the Lord had spoken to him, and Lot went forth with him. And Abram was seventy-five years old when he left Haran.'"

"Seventy-five?" said the boy. "Hangin' out in dad's basement a little too long, aren't we?" The old man chuckled as the boy asked, "Who was Lot again?"

"His nephew, whose father had died."

"Right," said the boy. "Let's hear it then."

"Well, Abram, his wife Sarai, his nephew Lot, and a few unnamed others from Haran set off toward the land of Canaan. But after a long journey they arrive to find the land already occupied. There was no welcome party after our chosen one entered the land of these cursed descendants of Noah. There was no comfort or acknowledgment for Abram's people. Instead, all we know is that 'the Lord appeared to Abram and sai—'"

"Hold up, hold up. What does that mean, the Lord *appeared*?"

"He, um…" said the man, scratching his head. "Well, to be honest, I'd never really given much thought to that line."

"Yeah, I noticed," said the boy. "You were about to gloss over it just like the author did. But other than Eden, God hasn't done much *appearing* before now. Is this a vision in Abram's mind? Was God some kind of hovering ghostly spirit? Did he manifest Himself in the classic old-man-with-a-beard-and-sandals type of way?"

"Well…" said the man, still searching for an answer.

"This seems like a pretty significant event, yet I'm the only one to take notice? Are they saying Abram got a good look at the Almighty and didn't care to spit out a few words on what He looked like?"

"Apparently not," said the old man. "And while the details aren't mentioned, we'll see God appear in numerous ways throughout the Scripture, some like the ones you mentioned, others like dreams, or a transference of thought, or a vision."

"Well, I guess we chalk it up to one of those mysteries we'll never solve then," said the boy.

With a nod the old man found his place again. "So the Lord appears to Abram and says, 'To your descendants I will give this land.' But Abram isn't discouraged by this unwelcoming arrival. Instead, he builds an altar for the Lord and prays. Then he moves on to the mountain east of Bethel and pitches his tent, and again he builds an altar to the Lord and calls on the name of the Lord."

"I assume there's some significance there?" said the boy.

"Oh yes," said the man. "The first time Abram builds an altar was after God appeared to him. But when Abram pitches his tent the following night, he builds an offering on his own accord, merely to honor God, and perhaps offer gratitude and prayer for their safe passage across the mountain. This becomes a ritual for Abram's family and their followers wherever they pitch their tents at night. A reminder that wherever we go, let us not forget our relationship with God."

The boy nodded quietly to allow the man's words to linger.

"Then they pack up and head south," said the man, reading on again:

> Now there was a famine in the land, and Abram went down to Egypt to live there for a while because the famine was severe. As he was about to enter Egypt, he said to his wife Sarai, "I know what a beautiful woman you are. When the Egyptians see you, they will say, 'This is his wife.' Then they will kill me but will let you live. Say you are my sister, so that I will be treated well for your sake and my life will be spared because of you."[23]

"I love the assumption he jumps to," said the boy, "even though he's never actually *been* to Egypt."

"What assumption is that?" said the man.

"That his wife is so hot she'll be desired by every Egyptian in town because apparently they only produce uggos there. Not to mention she's gotta be around seventy-five here." The old man's eyebrows perked up. "Not that there's anything wrong with being old," said the boy, "but come on now. The *Pharaoh* of Egypt, who can have his choice of any young pick of the litter in his own country, or Abram's caravan for that matter, is going to settle for a little old lady who's withering away after trudging through a desert? And they'd *murder* him for her? It's a tad presumptuous is all I'm saying."

"But they do—"

"I mean what kind of example is that setting for your followers anyway? Never mind your wife. You're God's *chosen one*. You have his *blessing*. Everyone who curses you will be cursed! Where is your confidence that God didn't march you across some unknown land just to be slaughtered at the time of your arrival? Ye of little faith, you might say. Honestly I think he was into the idea. Abram must've been the world's first cuckold."

There was a strong and awkward silence as the man turned to look off into the distance.

"Sorry," said the boy. "Keep going."

With a sigh the man turned back to his Bible and read on:

When Abram entered Egypt, the Egyptians saw that the woman *was* very beautiful. And when the princes of Pharaoh saw her, they praised her to Pharaoh. And the woman was taken into Pharaoh's house.[24]

"These Pharaohs are freaks."

"I can't do this," said the man, closing his Bible.

"No, no, wait. Come on, I'm just joking around." The old man stared off into the distance once again. "I'll stop, I promise. Here, where were we," said the boy, looking down at his own version. "They took her into the house and gave Abram many gifts in exchange. 'He had sheep and cattle and donkeys and male and female slaves and she-asses and camels. But the Lord afflicted Pharaoh and his household with terrible plagues because of Sarai the wife of Abram.'"

The old man maintained his stare.

"Come on, man, you're not even paying attention. Look, I was right. Obviously Abram screwed up if God's bringing plagues around."

"No," sighed the man, "God wasn't pleased with Abram's lie."

"Seems like Pharaoh wasn't too pleased here either," said the boy, looking down to read:

"What have you done to me? Why didn't you tell me she was your wife? Why did you say, 'She's my sister,' so that I took her as my wife? Now, here is your wife. Take her and go!" Then Pharaoh gave his men orders about him, and they sent him away with his wife and all he had.[25]

The boy looked skyward and shook his head in disbelief.

"What?" said the man.

"I take back what I said. I don't know what message God is trying to send here."

"What do you mean?"

"Well look what just happened. Abram lies and deceives to pimp out his wife and he's *rewarded* for doing so, all because poor Pharaoh is trying to win over Sarai's 'brother' for an honest marriage. And if it's not bad enough that Pharaoh is being duped, God sets a *plague* upon his innocent people? And while Pharaoh is coughing up blood or whatever, he tells Abram, 'Eh, just go along your merry way without any symptoms of this pandemic you caused. I won't slay you for bringing sickness and death upon my kingdom with your lies or anything.' It's pretty lame honestly. What moral are we supposed to take away here? Lie and deceive and God will help you escape with treasure?"

Taken aback, the man said, "Well that's certainly a different way of looking at things."

"Well how are you *supposed* to look at things?"

"First of all," said the man, "God certainly doesn't endorse lies and deceit. He spares Abram because of the covenant they have and tries him for this behavior later on. As for Pharaoh and his princes, I only saw them value Sarai as a sexual object to be taken into a bed chamber, as opposed to getting to know her inner beauty as a woman."

"We don't even know if Sarai *has* any inner beauty," said the boy. "She could be a terrible person for all we know, one that goes along with these mischievous plans her husband schemes up, like some kind of original Bonnie and Clyde. Instead of banks and guns they steal dowries with smallpox."

"I doubt this story is the way you're making it out to be," said the man. "We can hardly assume there was an ulterior motive here."

"What do you mean?" said the boy. "Abram said, 'Please say you are my sister, that it may be well with me for your sake.' Seems like he was after material gain from the start."

"Yes, 'and that I may *live* because of you,'" said the man. "I'd say the fear for his life was the greater concern here."

"Maybe," said the boy, "or maybe Abram was using fear as an excuse to convince Sarai to sleep with Pharaoh for material gain when clearly he already knew he had God's blessing. Let's see how things shake out because so far I'm not sold on Abram being as saintly as the rumors make him out to be."

The old man opened his Bible again and stared into the pages quietly. After a moment to himself he read on:

> Then Abram went up from Egypt, he and his wife and all that he had—

"*Stole*," said the boy.

The man squeezed his eyes shut for a moment before he kept reading:

> ...and Lot with him, to the South. Abram was very rich in live-stock, in silver, and in gold. And he went on his journey from the South as far as Bethel, to the place where his tent had been at the beginning, between Bethel and Ai, to the place of the altar which he had made there at first. And there Abram called on the name of the Lord.[26]

"Yeah, thanks, Lord, for all that treasure we robbed." The boy made his voice all dainty and feminine. "Oh, my. Woe is me. That big mean Pharaoh will kill me when he finds out I married a pretty lady!" With a fold of the arms he said, "Asshole."

The old man drew in a long breath and exhaled in the same manner before he tried to read again:

> Lot also, who went with Abr—

"You know, at least we can take away some kind of don't-judge-a-book-by-its-cover moral here. Pharaoh turned out to be a pretty nice guy. Even after Abram brought *plagues* upon his household he still sent them away with gold and silver. I mean Sarai must have made a real good impression on him." A smile grew upon the boy's face as he said, "Though I won't venture a guess as to how."

The man scrunched his face in dismissal and said, "We shouldn't assume anything happened between them."

"We shouldn't?" said the boy. "Pharaoh clearly said, 'I took her as a wife.' And he paid him for her, *well*, I might add. Clearly there was a transaction and clearly Pharaoh thought he got a pretty good deal. God set terrible plagues upon them *because* of Sarai, to put a stop to whatever *un*godly things she was doing in there."

The boy shook his head in a tsk tsk manner as the man said, "I don't think that's how the story goes," his frustration showing through.

"Suit yourself," said the boy, "but I think Pharaoh is the only saintly one in this tale. I don't understand why God punished him when he's the one who got tricked into paying for what he thought was a perfectly legitimate wife."

"Well, God works in mysterious ways," said the man.

"Oh don't give me that," said the boy. "Everyone knows that's a cop-out to justify unexplainable things."

"Well, perhaps if God had not created the plague that led Pharaoh to send them away, Abram would have stayed in Egypt, where things were easy, instead of pushing forth to live out God's plan. Not to mention he would have lost his wife completely." The boy said nothing, so the man pressed on. "And there's nothing that says this was a deadly plague. I think it's you filling in the blanks this time."

"That's fair," said the boy. "Plus the story would have come to an end too soon anyway."

"Maybe this was all to see the lesson you mentioned," said the man, "to experience the generosity and forgiveness of someone you unfairly judged." The boy gave a nod in silence, so the man read on:

> Now Lot, who went with Abram, also had flocks, herds, and tents. And the land could not support both of them while living together, for their possessions were so great that they were not able to remain together. And there was strife between the herdsmen of Abram's livestock and the herdsmen of Lot's livestock. Now the Canaanites and the Perizzites were living in the land at that time.[27]

> So Abram said to Lot, "Please let there be no strife between you and me, and between my herdsmen and your herdsmen, for we are brethren. Is not the whole land before you? Please separate from me. If you take the left, then I will go to the right, or if you go to the right, then I will go to the left."[28]

"Leave it to wealth to divide a family," said the boy.

The man stared off into the distance with a solemn nod. "Yes, my sister and I had a falling out over the will of our parents when they died." He coughed up a single, saddened laugh and said, "It was so foolish. We never spoke again, and now she's gone too. I'll never live that down." He shook his head as he looked back at the boy, who returned his gaze with compassion. "Abram, though, was wise in the way he dealt with Lot. He could have easily said, 'I'm your elder, so I'll choose the more fertile land for myself and leave you the dregs.' Who knows what might have happened then if there was already strife between the men. Perhaps the neighbors would've grasped the window to divide and conquer if they saw there was turmoil."

"That's true," said the boy. "But let's find what did happen."

So the man read on:

Lot took a long look at the fertile plains of the Jordan Valley in the direction of Zoar. The whole area was well watered everywhere, like the garden of the Lord or the beautiful land of Egypt.[29]

"Sounds like a pretty good choice to me," said the boy.

"Lot thought so too," said the man, reading on again:

Abram lived in the land of Canaan, while Lot lived among the cities of the plain and pitched his tents near Sodom. But the people of Sodom were wicked and were sinning greatly against the Lord.[30]

"Uh-oh," said the boy. "Here come your evil cities again."

"We shall see," said the man with a smile. "But I like this part at the close of the chapter. The Lord comes back to Abram and tells him that the land he's left with will be his forever, to explore it, to know that his descendants will multiply there. This fulfills the promise He made to Abram before he set out on his journey. And so Abram builds an altar, a good reminder that God deserves our praise when He delivers on His promises."

The boy gave a nod.

"It's worth noting also," said the man, "that God comes at a time when Abram has parted from his companion, undoubtedly a saddening time. Not to mention a time when the strength of his clan was cut in half. This serves as a reminder that communion with God may serve to fill any longing for lost or distant friends, and that when separated from our kin, He can give us the strength we need."

The boy agreed, but with a stark change in demeanor, he said, "Wait a minute. When they first introduced Sarai, didn't they say she was barren?"

"They did," said the man.

"So how are Abram's *descendants* supposed to…" The boy trailed off as the man failed to hold back a smile. "Never mind," said the boy. "I guess I'll wait and see."

Rehearsing from memory, the man said, "Then a war breaks out amongst the surrounding kings in the land where Lot chose to settle. There was an invasion and raid of the kingdoms of Sodom and Gomorrah, driving the survivors into the mountains.

The invaders plunder all the goods and provisions and take captives before they leave, Abram's nephew among them."

"Those damn cities," said the boy with a smile.

"But one of Lot's servants escapes to find Abram and reports the news. When Abram hears of this, he arms three hundred men and goes on the chase. He tracks them down and attacks them and is able to rescue Lot and all his people and belongings."

"It's interesting to hear God's chosen one isn't just some meditating man on a mountain or something, but instead a warrior who can lead an army into battle," said the boy, thrusting an imaginary sword at an invisible adversary.

"Very true," said the man, raising an index finger. "And not just conquest for the sake of gain either. He only drew the sword to rescue a friend in need."

"Not bad for a seventy-five-year-old who just moved out of his parents' basement," said the boy, sheathing his invisible sword.

The old man chuckled. "Anyway, the king of Sodom goes out to meet Abram as he returns from victory, and his ally, the king of Salem, brings bread and wine to celebrate and bless Abram. They try to hand Abram a reward, but Abram turns it down here," said the man:

"I have lifted my hand to the Lord, God Most High, Possessor of heaven and earth, that I would not take a thread or a sandal strap or anything that is yours, lest you should say, 'I have made

Abram rich.' I will take nothing but what the young men have eaten, and the share of the men who went with me.[31]

"How noble," said the boy, a hand over his heart, eyelashes fluttering.

The man continued:

After these things the word of the Lord came to Abram in a vision, saying, "Do not be afraid, Abram. I am your shield, your exceedingly great reward."

But Abram said, "Lord God, what will You give me, seeing I go childless, and the heir of my house is Eliezer of Damascus?"

Then Abram said, "Look, You have given me no offspring. Indeed one born in my house is my heir!"[32]

"Sheesh," said the boy. "This really seems to be weighing on him."

"Yes, well, although Abram has honor and glory and land and gold, it means nothing to him without an heir to pass it along to. It's noteworthy also that his first verbal speech to God is doubt that His promise can be delivered. Up until this point, all we've seen from Abram is silent obedience or gestures of gratitude."

"Yeah, I don't think God appreciated that. Seems like there was an awkward pause before Abram spat out another line *blaming* God for the lack of offspring." The boy coughed, "*Adam*," before he said, "Poor Sarai can't been feeling too pleased with herself here either."

"No, I can't imagine so. But God assures Abram with this," said the man:

> "This one shall not be your heir, but one who will come from your own body shall be your heir."
>
> Then He brought him outside and said, "Look now toward heaven and count the stars if you are able to number them. So shall your descendants be."
>
> And he believed in the Lor—[33]

"Sorry, I skimmed ahead here. But this is a strangely specific sacrifice God asks for. A three-year-old heifer, a three-year-old she-goat, a three-year-old ram, a turtledove, and a young pigeon? I mean, that's a quest on its own. And how is he supposed to know the age of all these things? And why is the turtledove the only thing allowed to be old and decrepit?"

"Well, he'd have a pretty good idea of age having herds of his own," said the man.

"This sounds like a witch's brew," said the boy, shifting his voice into a high-pitched whine. "Bring me four toadstools, three frog tongues, two bat wings, and a partridge in a pear tree!"

The man tried not to laugh, but a smile escaped him. "Well, right before this, Abram asks God how he'll know when he'll inherit the promised land, so God asks him to make this sacrifice, presumably in exchange for the sign Abram's looking for. The age of three is approximately when those animals are the healthiest and strongest, because God deserves the best in terms of our sacrifice. As far as the turtledove, you've got me there."

"Just one of those mysteries," said the boy.

"Just one of those mysteries," said the man. "But there's a part here worth mentioning, where Abram is awaiting his sign and has to scare away vultures that swoop down to pick at his sacrifice. This could be seen as a metaphor for batting away any doubts that surface in your mind while waiting for a sign from God."

"That makes sense," said the boy. "So what happens?"

So the old man read:

> Now when the sun was going down, a deep sleep fell upon Abram, and behold, horror and great darkness fell upon him.
>
> Then He said to Abram, "Know certainly that your descendants will be strangers in a land that is not theirs, and will serve them, and they will afflict them four hundred years."[34]

"Damn," said the boy, "all that journeying through strange lands, giving your wife up to Pharaohs, and fighting battles, all for the promise of your mysterious offspring to be slaves?"

"Well, God goes on to say, 'the nation whom they serve I will judge' and 'afterward they shall come out with great possessions.' And at least Abram 'shall go to your fathers in peace' and 'be buried at a good old age.'"

"Back to dad's basement?"

"No, no," laughed the man. "Fathers as in ancestors in the afterlife."

"Oh, duh. Alright, so Abram is lying there having a divine revelation. Then what?"

The man read on:

And it came to pass, when the sun went down and it was dark, that behold, there appeared a smoking oven and a burning torch that passed between those pieces.[35]

"An *oven*? Like a General Electric range top? What are we talking about here?"

"Well, I thi—"

"Look," said the boy, pointing at his text, "at least here it says a 'smoking brazier,' which can be lit with wood or something. I know they're trying to modernize the translations and all, but can't they assume the average reader is smart enough to realize we're talking olden times?"

"Well this could have been a coal oven. I've also heard the translation as 'firepot,'" said the man, "which is perhaps more in line with what's trying to be conveyed here."

"Anything's better than *oven*," said the boy. "The story is supposed to be wrapped in mysticism, and the imagery sucks you right out of it. All I'm saying is that we've just made a great sacrifice of turtledoves and heifers and now our sign is a smoking kitchen appliance we don't have a fire extinguisher for?"

"You seem really upset about the oven," said the man. "Is it something we can move past, or should we call it a day?"

"Oh shit, what time is it?" said the boy, looking at his watch. He slammed his book shut and stood abruptly.

"Another dinner?"

"No, no. I have a test tomorrow I haven't studied for." He stuffed the book in his bag and slung it over his shoulder. "Look, I'm not blaming God here. Clearly He delivered a lasting impression to symbolize the covenant. I just think the translator dropped the ball on this one."

The man shook his head with a smile.

"Alright, see you tomorrow," said the boy.

The old man raised his hand goodbye, but the boy had already turned down the path.

GENESIS 16-17

ABRAHAM & SARAH

Where have you come from, and where are you going?
—the angel of the Lord

"The man's in his eighties and she offers him a nice young servant to fertilize? He's probably thinking, *You don't have to tell me twice!*"

The man wrestled with a smirk as he said, "I'm not sure you'd get away with saying something like that in today's world."

"We're not *in* today's world," said the boy. "We're in a time when morals are still being ironed out. Keep going."

So the man read on:

Then Sarai, Abram's wife, took Hagar her maid, the Egyptian, and gave her to her husband Abram to be his wife.[36]

"Wait a minute. Back in Cain's line you were saying polygamy was evil. But now God's chosen one is allowed to have two wives?"

"Here's a lesson about what trouble it brings to the household," said the man.

"Yeah, but God still allowe—"

"*God* didn't propose this," said the man, "Sarai did. And Abram, as you astutely noticed, jumped on the opportunity."

"Literally. But Sarai just said, 'The Lord has restrained me from bearing children. Perhaps I shall obtain children by her.' And I thought Abram was supposed to get an heir soon?"

"Again, this is coming from Sarai," said the man. "And although God promised Abram descendants, He never said they should come from someone other than his wife."

"But she's barren…"

"At least she has been," said the man.

"I'm not sure I follow," said the boy, "but go ahead."

"So he goes in to Hagar and she conceives. And when she sees that she had conceived, her mistress becomes despised in her eyes."

"Jeez, Hagar, rub it in."

The man agreed and read on:

> Then Sarai said to Abram, "This is all your fault! I put my servant into your arms, but now that she's pregnant she treats me with contempt. The Lord will show who's wrong, you or me!"[37]

"Women!" said the boy. "Sheesh. Poor guy merely listens to his wife and it turns into the first domestic squabble. I don't know how you married people do it."

"Let's not throw all married people into the same box here," said the man. "Abram fell into temptation and now he's dealing with the consequences."

"Not to derail your point or anything," said the boy, "but it seems irrational that Sarai didn't take at least *some* responsibility, seeing as how it was her idea and all."

With a chuckle the man said, "Sounds like you're not getting married anytime soon, so that's nothing you need to worry about."

"Well," said the boy, "tell me what he said anyway."

"Abram says to Sarai, 'Indeed your maid is in your hand. Do to her as you please.' And when Sarai deals harshly with Hagar, she flees from her presence."

"I don't blame her for running away," said the boy. "I mean, I get she shouldn't have rubbed it in Sarai's face, but cut your pregnant slave a little slack here, won'cha? And Abram, man, what a sellout. He didn't exactly stand up for his new wife. Just chopped his balls off for the sake of peace with the first one. Are you sure this is the father of the chosen people or whatever?"

"Well, let's not gloss over that point you made about Sarai's responsibility. Although she allowed her husband to conceive with another woman, the relationship with Hagar was originally hers. Abram's response of '*your* maid is in *your* hand' seems to honor the respect he's had for Sarai all along. And considering the harsh accusations Sarai was throwing around, I'd say this was a pretty good way of handling things."

The boy nodded quietly. "You really were married, weren't you?"

"And perhaps there is another lesson in following God's will," said the man. "There's a parallel here with the garden, if you recall. After Sarai says, 'Please, go in to my maid,' the Bible says, 'And Abram heeded the voice of Sarai.' And when being expelled from Eden, God said to Adam, 'Because you have heeded the voice of your wife,' followed by his punishment."

"So the moral is never listen to your wife," said the boy with a smile.

"Not exactly," said the man. "These were times when the roles in marriage were a bit more fixed and imbalanced, sure, and Abram seems to have a more intimate relationship with the Lord than Sarai, but in today's world you can still apply the lesson of consulting God before heeding the advice of a spouse if you think they may be wrong."

"That makes sense," said the boy. "See? I had a feeling this book still had some wisdom for us."

"Oh yes," said the man. "Much of the wisdom in the Bible is timeless. How do you think it's outlasted kingdoms and empires?"

"Good point," said the boy. "Alright, let's see what else you've got."

So the man read on:

> Now the angel of the Lord found her by a spring of water in the wilderness, by the spring on the way to Shur. And He said, "Hagar, Sarai's maid, where have you come from, and where are you going?"
>
> She said, "I am fleeing from the presence of my mistress Sarai."
>
> The angel of the Lord said to her, "Return to your mistress, and submit yourself under her hand."[38]

"But when Hagar says nothing," said the man, "the angel tells her, 'I will multiply your descendants exceedingly, so that they shall not be counted for multitude.'"

"Yeah, the angel had to speak up twice because Hagar was so flabbergasted. First time an angel appears in the Bible and it's to tell a slave to get back to being a slave. Thanks, God."

"I would imagine it's more surprise," said the man. "Something akin to, 'Me? A humble servant should be so honored by the presence of God's first angel?' But if we can look past Hagar's unfortunate circumstance for a moment, we can see it was out of her control. But what was in her control was her reaction, mainly the gloating after being promoted from slave to wife by her own mistress. She thought she was a better woman than Sarai simply because she could conceive, and so she assumed Abram would favor her over his long-time wife. She let pride get the best of her, and when Sarai was left to deal with her, she couldn't bear it and ran away."

"There are so many more layers to these stories than I would've imagined," said the boy.

"These are only the ones I know of," said the man. "Who knows what other insights there are? But listen to the way the angel humbles her. He greets her by saying, 'Hagar, Sarai's maid,' to put her pride in check. Then He asks, 'Where have you come from, and where are you going?' which is a mighty good question for a pregnant woman then. What was her plan? Return to Egypt as a slave? Live in the wilderness on her own? Wander around until she's taken captive by strangers and raped or killed? Or should she swallow her pride and return to her home where there is wealth and food and community?"

"I guess those are pretty good questions," said the boy.

"We can entertain these simple-minded ideas such as, 'Why does the Holy Bible have slaves in the first place?' or we can examine the stories for what they are, given the context of the times, and try to gather any wisdom there might be."

"Alright," said the boy, "I hear what you're saying. Let's keep going."

So the man read the angel's next line:

"Behold, you are with child, and you shall bear a son. You shall call his name Ishmael, because the Lord has heard your affliction. He shall be a wild man. His hand shall be against every man, and every man's hand against him. And he shall dwell in the presence of all his brethren."[39]

"Sounds like a handful," said the boy.

"Yes," said the man, "well, she's told she must return to Abram, perhaps a sacrifice of her own freedom, but in doing so she secures the freedom of her son, who will go on to live as an independent and untamable man. In that case, she'll become the mother of countless future generations of free people."

"Well when you say it like that," said the boy, "sounds like a pretty important role."

"I agree," said the man, reading on again:

> Then she called the name of the Lord who spoke to her, You-Are-the-God-Who-Sees, for she said, "Have I also here seen Him who sees me?"[40]

"And so here we see an expression of awe that God not only watches over her, but also appears before her after she's run away, gracing her with His very presence. Humbled as she was, she returns to bear Abram his first son."

"Probably for the best," said the boy. "But this stirs the question, if God's ideal is monogamy, why did He restore polygamy to the chosen one's household?"

"What was He supposed to do," said the man, "leave her to the wolves?"

"I don't know, you tell me. He had no problem drowning everyone a few years ago. What's one more slave from a pagan culture? All I'm saying is this was a chance to show Abram that having two wives brings so much trouble that one of them will run away pregnant and leave you feeling guilty. Now *that's* a lesson. Instead, when Sarai restores the balance to a one-woman home, God says, 'Nah, I prefer it when Abram has two.' He even blesses this one as the future mother of free nations."

"I think He's merely doing what's best given the situation Abram has created for himself," said the man. "There's also the argument Hagar was just a surrogate, never really a wife. When the Scripture says Sarai gave her to be Abram's wife, it was probably a euphemism for the act of procreation. Here we see the angel of the Lord address Hagar as 'Sarai's maid,' not Abram's wife. Then He tells her to go back and submit to Sarai, not Abram. Sarai gave Hagar to Abram solely because she wanted children. Not something condoned by the Lord in this case, but not an uncommon practice in those times either. The point is, this was done without the counsel of God, and Sarai was the first to reap the bitter fruits of her decision."

"Mhm. Anyway," said the boy, "what's next?"

So the man looked down and read:

When Abram was ninety-nine years old, the Lord appeared to Abram and said to him, "I am Almighty God, walk before Me and be blameless. And I will make My covenant between Me and you, and will multiply you exceedingly. Then Abram fell on his face."[41]

"Fell on his face?"

"It means he bowed down in the presence of the Lord."

"Oh, I see. They kinda gloss over how it's been a decade since God 'appeared' again. Wouldn't have surprised me if he just keeled over at that age, simply out of relief his first encounters weren't hallucinations or something. That's a long time to hold on to the faith you didn't lead your people into a desert and pimp your wife out for nothing."

"Yes," said the man, "the timeline is a good observation. In such a concise story we may feel Abram's life is crowded with revelations, but these three divine occurrences span over twenty-five years. And perhaps the long delay on the part of the Lord was by design, chastising Abram's second marriage as undue haste."

"*Haste?*" said the boy. "The guy's almost a century old and God hadn't produced an heir! How long are you supposed to wait before taking matters into your own hands?"

"As long as the Lord expects you to wait is the answer to that question," said the man.

"I don't know if I'd have that kind of patience."

"Well, you're only human, but there may come a consequence for not following God's will. Anyway, God tells Abraham this," said the man:

"Behold, My covenant is with you, and you shall be a father of many nations. No longer shall your name be called Abram, but your name shall be Abraham, for I have made you a father of many nations."[42]

"Why the name change?" said the boy.

"In many countries, a change of name shows a new circumstance in the rank of the individual. Here the meaning of his name is changed from 'a high father' to 'a father of many,' for God is reassuring him that He will honor His covenant."

"Gotcha," said the boy.

"God also goes on to reassure Abraham that He will make him fruitful, that He will make nations of him, and that kings shall come from him. He reaffirms the everlasting covenant between Him and all his descendants, but in exchange God says, 'This is My covenant which you shall keep, between Me and you and your descendants after you, every male child among you shall be circumcised.'"[43]

"Whaaat?" said the boy. "*This* is where that comes from? I didn't realize it was so early on. They're still dwelling in tents at this point. Weren't they worried about sanitation?"

"Keep in mind," said the man, "the concept of germs wasn't known back then."

"And how are they going about this?" said the boy. "A rock? Do they even have knives?"

"The method isn't detailed," said the man, "but as it says in the next line, 'It shall be a sign of the covenant between Me and you.' And a couple lines later, 'My covenant shall be in your flesh for an everlasting covenant.' Which means this is their way to honor God in a permanent way."

"Who exactly has to get circumcised?" said the boy. "Only newborns?"

"Everyone," said the man. "Men, children, slaves, babies after eight days. As it says, for he 'who is not circumcised in the flesh of his foreskin, that person shall be cut off from his people, he has broken My covenant.'"

"But Abram's like a hundred," said the boy, scrunching his face. "That can't be good for you. And eight-day old babies?" The boy shivered.

"With this tradition the parent is helpless to watch," said the man, "and the child a passive recipient. But this is the first lesson for both in godly education, one where the parents acknowledge their obligation to raise their children in the way of God, and this is the formal admission of the child into the privilege of the covenant. This admission cannot be reversed except by a deliberate rebellion of the child later on."

"You know," said the boy, "this really begs the question, is God circumcised?" The man blinked and stared blankly. "Well, obviously if we were created in His image, He at least *had* a foreskin, right? But He doesn't have to make this covenant with Himself, does He? So why would He have to…" The boy trailed off as the man stared with a growing look of concern. "Never mind," said the boy. "Keep going."

The man hesitated a moment longer before reading:

Then God said to Abraham, "As for Sarai your wife, you shall not call her name Sarai, but Sarah shall be her name. And I will bless her and also give you a son by her. Then I will bless her, and she shall be a mother of nations. Kings of peoples shall be from her."[44]

"You're kidding me," laughed the boy. "She's gonna pop a kid out at a hundred?"

"You're not the only one with that reaction," said the man:

> Then Abraham fell on his face and laughed, and said in his heart, *Will a child be born to a man a hundred years old? And will Sarah, who is ninety years old, give birth to a child?*[45]

"I don't blame him," said the boy. "This keeps getting weirder."

"In a moment we'll see God names this future son Isaac, which means something akin to 'laughter,'" said the man, "named so because Abraham laughed out of joy."

"Or disbelief," said the boy.

"That's a fair assumption also," said the man. "But perhaps the Lord's power in this matter was magnified with Sarah's old age. Either way, it builds tension as the first man to laugh in the face of God."

"True," said the boy. "And so?"

"And so Abraham, as a father whose heart has clung to his firstborn of thirteen years, worries that God will have no grace for Ishmael in lieu of this foretold heir of Sarah's. And so Abraham says, 'Oh, that Ishmael might live before You!' And God responds with this," said the man:

> "No, but your wife Sarah will bear you a son, and you shall name him Isaac, and I will establish My covenant with him as an everlasting covenant for his descendants after him. As for Ishmael, I

have heard you. Behold, I will bless him, and make him fruitful and multiply him exceedingly. He shall father twelve princes, and I will make him into a great nation.[46]

"That was nice of God," said the boy.

"Yes, here we learn that we can be humbly free and open with God in our prayer, and that God will hear our woes." The boy nodded quietly. "Then, as parting words, God says, 'But My covenant I will establish with Isaac, whom Sarah shall bear to you at this set time next year,' and then He disappears." The man continued reading:

So Abraham took his son Ishmael and those born in his household or purchased, every male among the members of Abraham's household, and he circumcised the flesh of their foreskin on that very day, just as God had said to him.[47]

"Wow," said the boy. "Well *that* certainly paints an image. A hundred-year-old man bursts out of his tent and shouts, 'Gather' round, boys! God says I've gotta chop your dicks off!'"

"Well, I doubt that's how it wen—"

"Not gonna lie, at this point I'd start to wonder if he had dementia."

"I think we have to conside—"

"Can you *imagine*?" said the boy. "Abraham corralling every one of his men and going down a line one by one with a *knife*? Now that gives me the heebee-jeebees."

"I don't thin—"

"And there's no drugs or numbing agents or anything," said the boy. "After the first one, he just wipes the blood on his robe and on to the next. Poor fella at the end of the line has to witness a hundred men before him drop to the ground writhing in pain, blood squirting from their groins."

"That—"

"That would be enough to make me renounce my religion and run, I can tell you that much. No thanks, Abra-Scissorhands. I'm out!"

"Well—"

"And those poor *mothers*, man, breastfeeding their new-borns when some geezer with a bloody crotch comes limping up and says, 'I'm gonna need to borrow that baby!'"

"I really wish you'd stop describing it this way," said the man.

"What a lunatic!" said the boy. "Are you sure Stephen King didn't write this one? And what are they doing with the tips of all those penises? Just leaving them out for the wildlife to pick through?"

"Al*right*," said the man with growing impatience, "that's enough."

"Did you know that in order to clean the wound, priests used to suck the baby's d—"

"*That's* not something I wanna hear any more about," said the man. "Let's just skip to the next chapter."

"Hey, you brought it up, man. I don't see why we couldn't have just signed the covenant with a rainbow like last time."

GENESIS 18-19

SODOM & GOMORRAH

And they struck the men who were at the
doorway of the house with blindness.
—Genesis 19:11

"So in the heat of the day," said the man, "the Lord appeared to Abraham as he was sitting by his tent door." He looked down to his Bible and read:

> When he raised his eyes and looked, behold, three men were standing opposite him, and when he saw them, he ran from the tent door to meet them and bowed down to the ground, and said, "My Lord, if now I have found favor in Your sight, please do not pass Your servant by. Please let a little water be brought and wash your feet, and make yourselves comfortable under the tree, and I will bring a piece of bread, so that you may refresh yourselves. After that you may go on, since you have visited your servant."[48]

"I'm totally confused," said the boy. "Who are these guys?"

"First of all," said the man, "in this time and place, it was customary to rest from labor during high noon, as we see Abraham doing here. Second, because there were no inns or established places to rest like we have today, dwellers of the land would welcome travelers to join them for refreshments before moving on in the cool of evening. But Abraham recognized these travelers as three heavenly beings assuming human form, one of them being the Lord Himself."

"Uh-huh," said the boy. "And how does he know this if they look like regular men? Couldn't they just have been random strangers?"

"Whatever visual cue Abraham sees isn't detailed," said the man, "but this fact is revealed shortly."

"Alright," said the boy, "let's hear it then."

"Abraham humbly bows and invites them to be his guests, and they tell him, 'Do as you have said.' So Abraham hurries into the tent and tells Sarah, 'Quickly, make ready three measures of fine meal, knead it and make cakes.'"

"Yeah," said the boy, "chop-chop!"

The man rolled his eyes and read on:

Abraham ran to the herd, took a tender and good calf, gave it to a young man, and he hastened to prepare it. So he took butter and milk and the calf which he had prepared, and set it before them, and he stood by them under the tree as they ate.

Then they said to him, "Where is Sarah your wife?"[49]

"Ah, okay," said the boy, "there's the giveaway."

"Indeed. And at this point Sarah was behind the tent flap listening, so here's what Abraham told them," said the man:

"Here, in the tent."

And He said, "I will certainly return to you according to the time of life, and behold, Sarah your wife shall have a son."

Now Abraham and Sarah were old, well advanced in age, and Sarah had passed the age of childbearing. Therefore Sarah laughed within herself, saying, *After I have grown old, shall I have pleasure, my lord being old also?*

And the Lord said to Abraham, "Why did Sarah laugh, saying, 'Shall I surely bear a child, since I am old?' Is anything too hard for the Lord? At the appointed time I will return to you, according to the time of life, and Sarah shall have a son."[50]

"Looks like God didn't care for Sarah doubting His miracle-working skills," said the boy.

"No," said the man, "and Sarah digs herself even deeper by denying it when she says, 'I did not laugh,' for she was afraid. But God says, 'No, but you did laugh!'"

"Caught red-handed by the All Knowing," said the boy.

"She was," said the man, reading on again:

When the men got up to leave, they looked down toward Sodom, and Abraham walked along with them to see them on their way. Then the Lord said, "Shall I hide from Abraham what I am about to do? Abraham will surely become a great and powerful nation, and all nations on earth will be blessed through him. For I have chosen him, so that he will direct his children and his household

93

after him to keep the way of the Lord by doing what is right and just, so that the Lord will bring about for Abraham what he has promised him."[51]

"What's going on here exactly?" said the boy.

"Well, their mission down on earth was not only to grace Abraham and Sarah with their presence, but they had business to attend to as well, the nature of which God tells Abraham here." The man looked down and read:

"The outcry against Sodom and Gomorrah is so great and their sin so grievous that I will go down and see if what they have done is as bad as the outcry that has reached me. If not, I will know."[52]

"So Sodom and Gomorrah are nearby cities that are evil and need to be punished?" said the boy.

"Judged first," said the man. "But apparently God debates on whether or not he should reveal his intentions to Abraham. I suppose He's worried Abraham may influence His decision, which turns out to be true. God reiterates how Abraham is destined to be the great and mighty father of nations. Therefore, he has the interest of humanity in an act of retribution on Sodom. God also says, 'blessed in him shall be all the nations of the earth,' showing that all that concerns mankind, concerns Abraham when it comes to the dealings of mercy and judgment. So Abraham must teach his people to avoid the sins of the doomed cities and keep the way of the Lord."

"Why would God be worried about His decision being influenced though?" said the boy. "Seems like He's putting on a ruse *so* Abraham will step up and show concern about mercy and judgment."

The old man's eyes widened as he thought about it. With an agreeing nod, he looked down to read on:

Then the men turned away from there and went toward Sodom, but Abraham still stood before the Lord. And Abraham came near and said, "Would You also destroy the righteous with the wicked? Suppose there were fifty righteous within the city. Would You also destroy the place and not spare it for the fifty righteous that were in it? Far be it from You to do such a thing as this, to slay the righteous with the wicked, so that the righteous should be as the wicked, far be it from You! Shall not the Judge of all the earth do right?"

So the Lord said, "If I find in Sodom fifty righteous within the city, then I will spare all the place for their sakes."[53]

"So he bargains with God?" said the boy.

"That's not the extent of it. Here, listen," said the man:

Then Abraham answered and said, "Indeed now, I who am but dust and ashes have taken it upon myself to speak to the Lord. Suppose there were five less than the fifty righteous. Would You destroy all of the city for lack of five?"

So He said, "If I find there forty-five, I will not destroy it."

And he spoke to Him yet again and said, "Suppose there should be forty found there?"

So He said, "I will not do it for the sake of forty."[54]

"And Abraham continues to advance on God's concessions, again and again and again, until God says, 'I will not destroy it for the sake of ten.' And notice," said the man, "He did not cease granting until Abraham stopped asking. Only then did God go on His way and Abraham return to his place."

"Those poor remaining nine," said the boy, shaking his head. "So I guess the message here is that you can haggle God down to whatever you want?"

"Well," said the man, "at least that He's open to dialogue."

The boy nodded and opened a palm toward the Bible, so the man read on:

> The two angels entered Sodom in the evening as Lot was sitting in Sodom's gateway. When Lot saw them, he got up to meet them. He bowed with his face to the ground and said, "My lords, turn aside to your servant's house, wash your feet, and spend the night. Then you can get up early and go on your way."[55]

"He just sees them as travelers, right? Or does he recognize them as holy?"

"As far as we know they appear as men, but perhaps he recognized something divine or special about them, as we see he greets them with a bow. But they tell him, 'No, we will spend the night in the open square.' But he insists again, so they turn in and enter his home. There he prepares for them a feast and they dine."

"Looks like there's at least one good man in Sodom," said the boy.

The man smiled and read on:

Now before they lay down, the men of the city, the men of
Sodom, both old and young, all the people from every quarter,
surrounded the house. And they called to Lot and said to him,
"Where are the men who came to you tonight? Bring them out to
us that we may know them carnally."[56]

"Carnally?" said the boy.

"Carnally," said the man.

"What does that mean exactly?"

"You know," said the old man, blushing slightly, "*carnally.*"

"The whole town wants to fuck 'em?"

"Well!" said the man, scarlet now. "Let's just say they pro-
fess the wicked intention for which the city is named."

"Wait a minute," said the boy. "'Sodom' is a play on *sodo-
mize*? What kind of people is Lot hanging around with?"

"Sinners," said the man.

"The whole city though? Young and old?"

"I suppose it was something of an epidemic."

The boy shook his head in disbelief. "Alright, well, what
happens?"

The man looked down again to read:

Lot went outside to meet them and shut the door behind him and
said, "No, my friends. Don't do this wicked thing. Look, I have
two daughters who have never slept with a man. Let me bring

them out to you, and you can do what you like with them. But don't do anything to these men, for they have come under the protection of my roof."[57]

There was a long and awkward pause after the man stopped reading.

"What just happened?" said the boy, furrowing his brow. "A mob comes to his doorstep so he offers his virgin daughters to be raped instead of giving up strangers he's known for five minutes? What kind of book are you reading me?"

"Well," said the man, knotting his wrinkled fingers in his lap, "I've searched for some kind of reasonable explanation for this offering, but to be honest, I've found none that's satisfying."

"So it wasn't a joke, or like a distraction tactic or something?"

"The explanations I've found say it was something akin to trading a smaller sin for a greater sin."

"Feeding your daughters to wolves instead of some strangers is the lesser of two evils?"

"Well, you see, the laws of hospitality back then would have encouraged him to do his utmost to protect his guests."

"'The laws of hospitality'? That's the best you can come up with? What is with this family and pimping out loved ones?"

"I agree," said the man, "it's hard to know what to make of that. But I didn't write the book, my boy, that's just how it goes."

"Just," said the boy, pausing to rub the bridge of his nose, "keep going."

"Right, anyway, here's how the mob responds," said the man:

"Stand back!" Then they said, "This one came in to stay here, and he keeps acting as a judge. Now we will deal worse with you than with them." So they pressed hard against the man Lot, and came near to break down the door.

But the men reached out their hands and pulled Lot into the house with them, and shut the door. And they struck the men who were at the doorway of the house with blindness, both small and great, so that they became weary trying to find the door.[58]

"Blindness?" said the boy. "Wait a minute. So this whole story is some kind of moral about not sticking your you know what up other people's..."

The man's eyes opened wide, so the boy reconsidered his words.

"This is like that joke where the grandfather is telling his grandsons if you masturbate too much you'll go blind. Then the boys say, 'But, Grandpa, we're over here!'"

The old man burst out laughing so hard a tear came to his eye. "I never heard that one before."

"Really?" said the boy as the man gathered himself again. "It's a classic."

Wiping a tear under his eye the old man said, "I think what we're intended to take away is a moral about how to treat the strangers that cross your path in life, because you never know who you're dealing with."

"Right," said the boy, rolling his eyes. "The laws of hospitality or whatever. Just tell me what happens to the daughters."

So the man read on:

> Then the men said to Lot, "Have you anyone else here? Son-in-law, your sons, your daughters, and whomever you have in the city, take them out of this place! For we will destroy this place, because the outcry against them has grown great before the face of the Lord, and the Lord has sent us to destroy it."
>
> So Lot went out and spoke to his sons—[59]

"Wait, wait, wait. Two strangers come to his door claiming God sent them to *destroy* the city and he doesn't ask who they are or how they plan to go about it?"

"Well, he just witnessed them blind an angry mob with divine power," said the man. "Does he really need to ask? And now that we've seen the dangers of immediate sexual gratification in a place where social structure has collapsed, would you stick around?"

"I guess not," said the boy. "Go ahead then."

"So Lot goes out and speaks to his sons-in-law and tells them, 'Get up, get out of this place, for the Lord will destroy this city!' But his sons-in-law think he's joking."

"I'm not sure what's more unbelievable," said the boy, "the fact that Lot was so eager to offer up his married daughters, or that their sodomizing husbands hadn't *known* them even after marriage."

"I think there's an implication of more than two daughters, but the ones married to the unbelieving sons-in-law perish with their husbands, while the two you're thinking of escape with Lot. Here, listen," said the man:

> When the morning dawned, the angels urged Lot to hurry, saying, "Arise, take your wife and your two daughters who are here, lest you be consumed in the punishment of the city."[60]

> When Lot still hesitated, the angels seized his hand and the hands of his wife and two daughters and rushed them to safety outside the city, for the Lord was merciful.

> When they were safely out of the city, one of the angels said, "Run for your lives! And don't look back or stop anywhere in the valley! Escape to the mountains, or you will be swept away!"[61]

"Leaving daughters behind would certainly explain why he lingered," said the boy. "Not to mention the home he's built over the years with all his stuff."

"I suppose this serves as a lesson for questioning whether or not you're in a place in life that's so bad you should leave and never look back, even if that place is your home."

The boy gave a silent nod as he mulled that over.

"Fortunately for Lot, the Lord was merciful and made that decision for him," said the man, reading on again:

> But Lot said to them, "No, my lords, please! Your servant has found favor in your eyes, and you have shown great kindness to me in sparing my life. But I can't flee to the mountains. This disaster will overtake me, and I'll die."[62]

"What is he afraid of in the mountains?"

"Perhaps frailty in old age," said the man, "but whatever it is, it shows doubt in the Lord's ability to provide strength and protection as he pleads to flee to a nearby city instead."

"You think he'd take the advice for high ground knowing God has a thing for floods," said the boy. "Anyway…"

"Anyway, here's the response," said the man:

"Behold, I grant you this favor also, that I will not overthrow the city of which you have spoken. Escape there quickly, for I can do nothing till you arrive there." Therefore the name of the city was called Zoar.[63]

"Why," said the boy, "what's that mean?"

"A place of refuge, or sanctuary," said the man, reading on again:

The sun had risen over the earth when Lot came to Zoar. Then the Lord rained brimstone and fire on Sodom and Gomorrah from the Lord out of heaven, and He overthrew those cities, and all the surrounding area, and all the inhabitants of the cities, and what grew on the ground. But Lot's wife, from behind him, looked back, and she became a pillar of salt.[64]

"A pillar of salt?" said the boy.

"In oriental countries it's customary for the wife to walk behind her husband, so we can assume this was her position then, perhaps lingering a bit too far behind both physically and meta-

phorically. Looking back as the men warned them not to diso-
beyed a direct order of God and showed her longing to return to
a sinful place. When she turned to face the brimstone and fire
raining down upon the earth, she must have been stifled by sul-
furous vapors, her body encrusted with salt that encapsulated her
like a statue. If this was her fate, while Lot made it safely just a
few paces ahead, we know how narrowly the rest of his family
escaped."

"She certainly got what she deserved for caring about those
stupid *daughters* left behind," said the boy, rolling his eyes.

"Yes, well..." the man trailed off absently. "Soon after seeing the smoke of the land roll up in the sky, Lot went out of Zoar
and lived in the mountains, for he was afraid to dwell in a city
after such a display. Then he and his two remaining daughters
lived in a cave."

"Jeez, now that his wife dies he's feeling brave enough to
climb into the mountains?"

"Sometimes paths of our own choosing, ones in which we
don't follow God's, can prove unsettling. Here is a lesson that
it's okay if disappointment in choosing our own way finally
leads us to the path God has chosen for us."

"That or all the fire in the valley smoked him out," said the
boy.

"Either way, we can see that a man who once had so much
wealth he could no longer live beside his uncle now had too

much pride to seek shelter with Abraham again. Instead he chose to dwell in some miserable cave with his daughters."

"Father of the year right there," said the boy.

"Well I doubt you're going to like this then," said the man, reading on:

> Now the firstborn said to the younger, "Our father is old, and there is no man on the earth to come in to us as is the custom of all the earth. Come, let us make our father drink wine, and we will lie with him, that we may preserve the lineage of our father."[65]

"You're kidding me..."

"I'm not," said the man, reading further:

> So they made their father drink wine that night. And the firstborn went in and lay with her father, and he did not know when she lay down or when she arose. It happened on the next day that the firstborn said to the younger, "Indeed I lay with my father last night. Let us make him drink wine tonight also, and you go in and lie with him, that we may preserve the lineage of our father."[66]

"Good Lord. What is in this wine that makes everyone wanna f—" the boy caught himself "—*lay with* their fathers? I'm surprised it's not illegal after that."

"Well, I'm certainly not condoning the behavior," said the man, "but I've sought answers to the same questions you've asked. What I've found is sympathy for their actions out of desperation, or perhaps recognition of their ignorance. Their father had no sons, they had no husbands, their mother and the rest of their family were dead, and they may never see another man again for all they knew. And so perhaps they thought these extreme circumstances would excuse this irregularity. And maybe this story highlights an echoing reminder that whatever was happening in Sodom followed Lot out of the city and caught him with his guard down."

"More like his pants down," said the boy. "I understand desperate times call for desperate measures, but preserving the lineage of your father doesn't seem like a valid excuse. Is this a normal response to have a salt pillar for a mother, or something they picked up in Zoar? I mean, where do virgin children learn such behavior? Maybe you're right about cities being evil after all."

"It seems their principles were so corrupted by contact with the people of Sodom that they were prepared to commit an act of incest," said the man. "Sometimes good intentions are abused to justify bad actions."

"I have to say, this is not what I expected in the first few pages of the *Holy* Bible."

"Remember," said the man, "the Bible is as much a guide how *not* to live as it is one how to."

"Tell that to the caveman who thinks his virgin daughters conceived by miracle. What a turnaround from feeding them to the mob," said the boy. "Maybe God should've just left the whole family in Sodom."

"Maybe, but that's not how the story goes. Here, listen," said the man, reading on:

> They made their father drink wine that night also. And the younger arose and lay with him, and he did not know when she lay down or when she arose. Thus both the daughters of Lot were with child by their father. The firstborn bore a son and called his name Moab, he is the father of the Moabites to this day. And the younger, she also bore a son and called his name Ben-Ammi, he is the father of the people of Ammon to this day.[67]

"And they grow up to become leaders?" said the boy. "Did the law of genetics not exist then? What's happening right now? I'm so confused…"

"Regarding that matter, I'm unsure," said the man, "but I think considering how little the Scripture speaks of Lot moving forward, we can at least take away that as much as drunkenness makes you forget, it can also make you forgotten."

GENESIS 20-21

ABIMELECH

Indeed you are a dead man because of
the woman whom you have taken,
for she is a man's wife.
—God

"So Abraham journeys to the South and stays in Gerar."

"Wait, why did he leave?"

"Perhaps it was a desire to get away from the destruction of the cities," said the man, "but we really don't need a reason for moving on. Abraham's purpose is to migrate from place to place on account of his herds, but also to explore and take possession of the land as God intended. Canaan was not his place for permanent settlement, only pilgrimage."

"I see," said the boy.

With reservation, the man read the next line:

Now Abraham said of Sarah his wife, "She is my sister." And Abimelech king of Gerar sent and took Sarah.[68]

The boy shook his palms at the sky as he yelled, "God's chosen people are *swingers*!"

"Pipe down," said the man, shoulders by his ears as he gazed around. "Someone could hear you."

The boy whispered, "Sorry," as he looked around himself. When he saw no one else around he said, "But at this point you can't even deny it. First she sets him up with Hagar, then he hooks her up with Pharaoh, and now here we are again, with no objection from Sarah, I might add, after that jolly good time she had at Pharaoh's house."

With impatience the man said, "Hagar was as a surrogate because Sarah was barren. The encounter with Pharaoh was a means of survival. And you'll see how Abimelech is punished soon enough."

"Well, what excuse do they have for the whole sister charade this time?" said the boy. "God even told him, 'I am your shield.' This is a slap in God's face if he doesn't trust Him by now."

"Yes, clearly Abraham still lacks faith and is acting out of fear again," said the man. "The Scripture is impartial when it comes to revealing the blemishes of its most celebrated heroes. Even diamonds have their flaws."

"*Flaws?*" said the boy. "Don't give me that. At this point we know Abraham is a fearless warrior with an army that can conquer kingdoms. What we have going on here is some good old-fashioned kinkery."

"I can assure you the Holy Bible does *not* condone extramarital affairs," said the man. "As we learned in Genesis, a man shall be joined to his wife and they shall become *one* flesh."

"Yeah, but if we're supposed to hold onto everything that happened before the fall, then shouldn't we all be naked, hanging around gardens without jobs, strictly eating from trees while we wait for God to pull out our ribs to make monogamous wives? Unless you're saying all those things still apply, we can't just cherry-pick this thing or that while *everything* else has changed. Before the fall we were naked, after the fall we were clothed. Before the fall we were vegans, after the fall we ate meat. Before the fall we were created from earth and ribs, after the fall we were born to men and women. Before the fall there was one monogamous couple, after the fall... what, we're supposed cling to this single arbitrary rule? That doesn't make any sense. The story doesn't show God's ideal is monogamy. It only reveals the circumstance in which creationism got us started. Allegedly," said the boy. "But I'm just not seeing anything against a little side flesh down here on earth. If God didn't care for this type of behavior, He would have made Abraham give back all his treasure in Egypt. Instead, His chosen couple goes on swinging left and right without backlash."

The man rolled his eyes. "If you insist that the issues his women are causing at home and summoned *plagues* aren't considered backlash, then I have nothing more to say. And if you're not convinced yet, there are plenty more rules and examples coming."

"Eh," the boy swatted his hand at the air, "both those things came from a lack of communication. But I'm listening."

"Keep in mind," said the man, "a distinguishing feature of the Bible is that it insists upon perpetual upward progress, raising men to be better and holier than those who came before them. What it doesn't do is disproportionately raise these characters above the level of their own time. Also keep in mind, it's possible even good men cannot only fall into sin, but relapse into the same sin again."

The boy remained silent, so the man read on:

And Abimelech king of Gerar sent and took Sarah. But God came to Abimelech in a dream by night, and said to him, "Indeed you are a dead man because of the woman whom you have taken, for she is a man's wife."[69]

The man looked up and raised his eyebrows for emphasis, but the boy merely raised his own as a mocking mirror, so he read on:

But Abimelech had not come near her, and he said, "Lord, will You slay a righteous nation also? Did he not say to me, 'She is my sister'? And even she herself said, 'He is my brother.' In the integrity of my heart and innocence of my hands I have done this."[70]

"Bonnie and Clyde, man, I'm telling you."

The man shook his head and kept reading:

And God said to him in a dream, "Yes, I know that you did this in the integrity of your heart. For I also withheld you from sinning against Me, therefore I did not let you touch her. Now therefore, restore the man's wife, for he is a prophet, and he will pray for you and you shall live. But if you do not restore her, know that you shall surely die, you and all who are yours."[71]

"Ahhh, the old 'surely die' trick again," said the boy. "Wonder what it means this time."

The man said, "May I just finish this part of the story please?" glaring up from the Bible.

"Sorry," said the boy. "Go ahead."

So the man did:

Abimelech rose early in the morning, called all his servants, and told all these things in their hearing, and the men were very much afraid. And Abimelech called Abraham and said to him, "What have you done to us? How have I offended you, that you have brought on me and on my kingdom great sin? You have done deeds to me that ought not to be done."[72]

The man looked up from the text and said, "I think that makes it *very* clear that taking another man's wife is a great sin. The Pharaoh knew it, Abimelech knew it, and now these themes seem to be universal."

"Well, taking another man's wife without intentions and consent all around maybe. But these guys were *duped* into sin by a chronic liar with a secret fetish."

The man peered skeptically out of the corner of his eye. "Why are you so caught up with this anyway?"

The boy glanced down and away. "I'm not." Then he pointed to the Bible and said, "I just think that book has been used to condemn a lot of things, and I want to make sure we're getting the story straight."

"Well, if you were listening, it said Abimelech *took* Sarah, presumably by force. It can hardly be assumed that Abraham and Sarah cared for this intrusion on their marriage."

"See, that's exactly what I'm talking about," said the boy. "You can't just stick *presumably* in a sentence and make it true. *Presumably* Abimelech was the most handsome man in all the land. And *presumably* Sarah longed for another go in the sheets with a rich and powerful man like Pharaoh. See? Your assumptions are just as valid as the ones I made up now."

"Let's just finish this part of the story," said the man. "We'll never agree on this." And without waiting for the boy's response, he read on:

> And Abimelech asked Abraham, "What was your reason for doing this?"[73]
>
> Abraham said, "Because I thought, surely there is no fear of God in this place, and they will kill me because of my wife."[74]

"She's a *hundred* years old," said the boy. "What, did they have great plastic surgery back then? None of this makes any sense."

"Though Sarah was ninety years old," said the man, "we have to take into account a few things. One, in this age of the world, men and women lived longer, so they didn't as soon decay. Two, she has retained her beauty because she hasn't endured the bearing and nursing of children. And three, God has blessed and rejuvenated her with the strength and youth required to bear children once more." The man paused to see if the boy had anything to say. When he didn't, he added, "And if you've listened carefully, we don't know the motivation for *why* Abimelech took her. Perhaps it wasn't her beauty, but rather to align himself with a rich nomadic warrior by marrying his sister."

"Whatever," said the boy. "Let's just get through this chapter. I don't have the patience for this."

"Fine," said the man, reading Abraham's next line:

"But indeed she is truly my sister. She is the daughter of my father, but not the daughter of my mother, and she became my wife."[75]

The boy's head collapsed forward and hit the table with a thud. A muffled voice emerged from his face-plant. "Tell me God's chosen people don't descend from incest."

"There were larger allowances for marriages then," said the man, resuming Abraham's line:

"And when God caused me to wander from my father's house, I said to her, 'This is the kindness you must do me. At every place to which we come, say of me, "He is my brother."'"

> Then Abimelech took sheep and oxen, and male and female servants, and gave them to Abraham, and returned Sarah his wife.[76]

"What is happeninggg?" came a muffled cry as the boy lifted his head and banged it down again. "What is wrong with everyone? Please," said the boy, looking up at the man this time. "*Please,* tell me there's a twist at the end where this is Satan's work and the real God comes down to smite these people."

"I cannot. But here's Abimelech's next line," said the man:

> "Behold, my land is before you. Dwell where it pleases you."
>
> To Sarah he said, "Behold, I have given your brother a thousand pieces of silver. It is a sign of your innocence in the eyes of all who are with you, and before everyone you are vindicated."[77]

"Giving her brother-husband silver is their way of vindication? Was everyone a product of incest then? What is wrong with their brains?"

"This gift was meant to clear her name in a way that warded off public disapproval for anyone who thought she may have lain with another man. And Abimelech was doing these things because God told him Abraham was a prophet, and that he would pray for him. So it was in looking out for his own best interest that he sent him away with gifts."

"How is Abraham supposed to learn a lesson about pimping out his wife if God rewards him every time he does it? This book is making less and less sense the more we read. I don't know if I can continue at this point, honestly."

"Just stick with it," said the man, reading on before the boy could object any further:

So Abraham prayed to God and God healed Abimelech, his wife, and his female servants. Then they bore children, for the Lord had closed up all the wombs of the house of Abimelech because of Sarah, Abraham's wife.[78]

The man looked up and said, "So you see? God had made Abimelech sick, or perhaps impotent, to prevent his sins. The gifts were a way of ensuring Abraham's prayer for their healing."

"But you said the Holy Bible doesn't condone extra-marital affairs."

"That's right," said the man. "I did."

"But God rewards Abimelech with children from both his wife *and* servants. He even agrees that his actions were out of the 'integrity of his heart.' Seems like God's issue was with taking Abraham's wife away, adding an already married woman to the harem of a man with integrity, not polygamy itself."

"Well, of course God takes issue with Abraham losing his wife, as we already saw in Egypt, but polygamy is having more than one wife. Abimelech only had one wife."

"So you can sleep with more than one person if you only marry one of them?"

"Of course not," said the man. "Abimelech is pagan, so none of this applies."

"So some innocent women and a God-fearing pagan are made impotent and forced to cough up silver and livestock to an incestuous prophet who weasels out of deception by justifying half-truths and they go on to become poly neighbors in Polyland where poly rules only apply to people who break them but not others. Am I getting this right?"

"Well…" said the man.

"You'd better keep reading," said the boy, "because if we stop now, I'm not sure I'll be back tomorrow."

"Happy to," said the man. "The coming chapters reveal how God deals with Abraham anyway." Then he read on again:

> And the Lord visited Sarah as He had said, and the Lord did for Sarah as He had spoken.

"Wait a minute. What does it mean the Lord *visited* and the Lord *did*? Is He getting in on the action now too?" The man frowned. "What? Abraham's a hundred. Maybe he needed a little help."

"Don't be ridiculous," said the man, looking down at his book again:

> And Sarah conceived and bore Abraham a son in his old age at the time of which God had spoken to him. Abraham called the name of his son who was born to him, whom Sarah bore him, Isaac. And Abraham circumcised his son Isaac when he was eight days old, as God had commanded him.[79]

The boy stared at the old man looking defeated. "He 'deals' with Abraham by providing him with the son he's always wanted? What kind of punishment is that?"

The man ignored this and read on:

> Abraham was a hundred years old when his son Isaac was born to him. And Sarah said, "God has made laughter for me, everyone who hears will laugh over me." And she said, "Who would have said to Abraham that Sarah would nurse children? Yet I have borne him a son in his old age." And the child grew and was weaned. And Abraham made a great feast on the day that Isaac was weaned.[80]

"Weaned?"

"Off breastmilk," said the man. "It shows a few years have passed by where the child grew healthy."

"Ah. Got it," said the boy.

So the man read on:

> Now Sarah saw the son of Hagar the Egyptian, whom she had borne to Abraham, mocking Isaac. Therefore she said to Abraham, "Drive out this slave woman and her son, for the son of this slave woman shall not be an heir with my son Isaac!"[81]

"Uh-oh," said the boy. "Payback."

"Yes, well, if Ishmael had behaved instead of mocking, or his mother before him gloating, perhaps Sarah would not have reacted so severely. But they abused their privilege of living amongst Abraham's family as free people, and so they forfeited that privilege."

The boy nodded, so the man went on:

This upset Abraham because Ishmael was his son. But God told Abraham, "Do not be upset over the boy and your servant. Do whatever Sarah tells you, for Isaac is the son through whom your descendants will be counted. But I will also make a nation of the descendants of Hagar's son because he is your son, too."[82]

So Abraham rose early in the morning and took bread and a skin of water and gave it to Hagar, putting it on her shoulder, along with the child, and sent her away. And she departed and wandered in the wilderness of Beersheba.[83]

The man looked up to see the boy staring at him, blinking wildly, so he cocked his head to the side.

"No, no," said the boy. "Totally normal that she just wanders off into the wilderness to live happily ever after."

"The dismissal of his wife and son were no doubt distressing for all parties involved," said the man, "but bear in mind, Hagar has now obtained her freedom, and Ishmael was of an age where it's not uncommon to be independent. Though they were no longer in the presence of God's chosen one, they still had the blessing of being His people. Although, we do see that faith tested as their water runs out and she lies a famished Ishmael under a shrub to shade him from the heat."

"Let's hear it then," said the boy.

So the man read on:

Then she went off and sat down about a bowshot away, for she thought, *I cannot watch the boy die.* And as she sat there, she began to sob.

God heard the boy crying, and the angel of God called to Hagar from heaven and said to her, "What is the matter, Hagar? Do not be afraid. God has heard the boy crying as he lies there. Lift the boy up and take him by the hand, for I will make him into a great nation."

Then God opened her eyes and she saw a well of water. So she went and filled the skin with water and gave the boy a drink.[84]

"She didn't see it before?"

"Oftentimes emotion blinds us to the remedy of a problem right before our eyes. Here we also have the Lord's reassurance that He will fulfill his promise, even when things look dire. Things may take longer to develop than we prefer, or fulfilled in ways we wouldn't imagine, but here is a reminder that He is with us even when we're ready to give in."

"So I take it things turned out alright then?"

The man nodded:

God was with the boy, and he grew, and he lived in the wilderness and became an archer. He lived in the wilderness of Paran, and his mother took a wife for him from the land of Egypt.[85]

"Sounds like it," said the boy.

"Indeed so. But from there we return to the story of Abraham," said the man, reading on:

Abimelech said, "God is with you in everything you do. Now swear to me here before God that you will not deal falsely with me or my children or my descendants. Show to me and the country where you now reside as a foreigner the same kindness I have shown to you."[86]

"And Abraham says, 'I will swear.' But then he brings up a situation where some of Abimelech's servants seized a well from his men."

"Is there significance that links these two well stories together?" said the boy.

"That's a good question," said the man. "Perhaps to highlight the importance of water as a means of survival in these dry countries, how they can mean life and death when you're alone or cause strife when surrounded by others. These men obviously recognize this as we see when Abimelech says, 'I do not know who has done this thing, you did not tell me, nor had I heard of it until today.' So they make a covenant to solidify their relationship, and in doing so, Abraham offers Abimelech sheep and oxen as a gesture to treat each other agreeably moving forward. But then he sets aside another seven sheep from the flock by themselves, so Abimelech asks, 'What is the meaning of these seven ewe lambs which you have set by themselves?'"

"Yes, Abraham," said the boy. "My question exactly."

"He says, 'You will take these seven ewe lambs from my hand, that they may be my witness that I have dug this well.' In other words," said the man, "Abraham is, in effect, buying back the rights to his own well. And after the dispute of the well is settled, Abraham names the place Beersheba, meaning 'well of oaths' to honor the place in which their covenant was made. And once Abimelech returns to the land of the Philistines with his army, Abraham plants a tamarisk tree in Beersheba."

"I assume there's some kind of symbolism for this?"

"Oh yes," said the man. "Tamarisk trees can grow to great size in a desert climate when they have a reliable water source, so it becomes a landmark of this important location, one we'll see again as Genesis unfolds. This also appears to be a literal representation of Abraham putting down roots, and as the text goes on to tell us, he stays in the land of the Philistines for a long time."

"Abimelech had quite the opposite reaction as Pharaoh," said the boy.

"Yes, obviously Abimelech was a God-fearing man himself and respected Abraham as a prophet if he allowed the practice of a foreign religion by his new neighbor. And we'll see Abraham continue that tradition wherever he goes, as he neither neglects nor is ashamed of his worship of the Lord."

GENESIS 22-24

ISAAC

Here I am.
—Abraham

"In time, God tested Abraham," said the man, reading aloud:

He said to him, "Abraham!"

And he said, "Here I am."

He said, "Take your son, your only son Isaac, whom you love, and go to the land of Moriah, and offer him there as a burnt offering on one of the mountains of which I shall tell you."[87]

"This usually involved slaughtering an animal," said the man, looking up from his Bible, "then burning it on an altar until it was consumed by flames."

The boy stared back at him with his mouth wide open. "After all that? But... I..." He stumbled around a bit before landing on, "This isn't exactly a bedtime story you've put together here, is it? If this is a joke, God sure has a pretty messed-up sense of humor."

"As I said before, I didn't write it," said the man. "But in asking Abraham first to leave his home, the Lord tested whether or not his love was greater for his father. Then by asking him to sacrifice his son, He's testing whether or not his love was greater for his child. That is to say, was earthly love or heavenly obedience stronger?"

"He obviously didn't have to test Abraham's regard for his wife," said the boy.

"I'll come back to that," said the man. "Here, Abraham rose early in the morning and—"

"Wai-, wai-, wai-, wai-, wait," said the boy, pumping his hand in the air accordingly. "That's it? The guy waits a century for an heir, and after kicking his firstborn out into the wild, he doesn't even hesitate to burn his only other kid alive? Like even a little bit?" The boy paused to rub the stress out of his eyes while he pieced together his thoughts. "At least with Ishmael he showed a bit of reluctance. But here, nothing?"

"It's true," said the man, "this is certainly a dilemma."

"A *dilemma..*?" said the boy.

"Does he listen to God's will," asked the man, "the very thing that has carried him this far? Will God ask for human sacrifice moving forward? How does this all align with the promise of Isaac growing up to found nations? And then there's Sarah. Surely she would disown him, and likely denounce his God. How could he ever return home with the blood of his own son on his hands?"

"Yeah, but he doesn't exactly *ask* those questions, now does he?"

"Those who follow God's will heartily will do so speedily," said the man, "before doubt creeps in and hinders progress in duty. It's likely he also wanted Sarah to know nothing about this journey, in case she tried to stop him."

"You... Why..." The boy stumbled around a bit more before settling on, "Never mind. Just keep reading."

So the man did:

Early the next morning Abraham got up and loaded his donkey. He took with him two of his servants and his son Isaac. When he had cut enough wood for the burnt offering, he set out for the place God had told him about. On the third day Abraham looked up and saw the place in the distance.[88]

"Poor Sarah, man. She wakes up one morning to find her family gone for the weekend, then her husband comes back alone with blood on his robe."

The man gave away no emotion as he kept reading:

Abraham said to his young men, "Stay here with the donkey. The boy and I will go over there to worship, then we'll come back to you." Abraham took the wood for the burnt offering and laid it on his son Isaac. In his hand he took the fire and the knife, and the two of them walked on together.[89]

"What's going through your mind as one of these men?" said the boy. "Your fearless leader is marching the darling future of civilization up a mountain at knifepoint, making him carrying his own bundle of firewood, using the same knife he once used to slice a piece of your dick off, and no one cares to ask, 'So what's the plan with that book of matches?'"

"Note how this is done in reflection of the manner in which Christ was forced to carry his own cross up the mountain," said the man.

"Let's save the New Testament for when the time comes," said the boy.

"That's fine," said the man. "But keep in mind the parallels between the stories. Sacrificing the son is another."

"I see what you're saying," said the boy. "Just tell me if it ends the same way."

The man gave a nod and read on:

But Isaac spoke to Abraham his father and said, "My father!"
And he said, "Here I am, my son."
Then he said, "Look, the fire and the wood, but where is the lamb for a burnt offering?"[90]

"Jeeez-usss," the boy groaned as he clapped his hands over his face.

"Should we stop?" asked the man.

"Should we stop?" said the boy, revealing a look of horror. "The first words the boy mutters are, 'Where is the lamb?' and you ask me if we should *stop*? Are you people dead inside? *This* is the book you worship?"

"I'm not sure if I should take offense to that 'you people' commen—"

"For Christ's sake, man, just tell me what happens!"

"Alright, alright." So the man read on:

Abraham answered, "God himself will provide the lamb for the burnt offering, my son." And the two of them went on together.[91]

"Then, after many a weary step," added the man as his finger paused from sliding across the line, "and with a heavy heart, 'they came to the place of which God had told him.'"

"Where are you getting that from?" said the boy, quickly scanning his own text. "Did you skip over a line where tears well up in his eyes or something? This guy is as stone-cold as Hannibal Lecter!"

"Well, we already know how torn Abraham was from sending his first son away. I think we can infer that a man who's about to sacrifice his only other son to God would do so with a heavy heart."

"I think we can infer any sane human being would have taken that request and told God to shove it up His a—"

"*Abraham* builds an altar then," said the man, "and places the wood in order. Then he binds Isaac his son and lays him upon the wood. Then Abraham stretches out his hand and takes the knife to slay his son."

"Without hesitation? Without remorse? The chosen one is a psychopath!"

"But the angel of the Lord calls from heaven to stop him," said the man, reading on:

"Abraham, Abraham!"

So he said, "Here I am."

And He said, "Do not lay your hand on the lad, or do anything to him, for now I know that you fear God, since you have not withheld your son, your only son, from Me."[92]

"Well, that's a relief," said the boy. "God was certainly right to test him and see if he has any wits left now that he's a hundred. Go ahead and read the part where God strikes him down with lightning because he's absolutely insane."

The man smiled and read on:

Then Abraham lifted his eyes and looked, and there behind him was a ram caught in a thicket by its horns. So Abraham went and took the ram, and offered it up for a burnt offering instead of his son. And Abraham called the name of the place, The-Lord-Will-Provide, as it is said to this day, "In the Mount of The Lord it shall be provided."[93]

"More like The-Lord-Will-Put-A-Stop-To-Madness," said the boy, but the man ignored him and kept reading:

Then the angel of the Lord called to Abraham a second time out of heaven and said, "By Myself I have sworn, says the Lord, because you have done this thing, and have not withheld your son, your only son, blessing I will bless you, and multiplying I will multiply your descendants as the stars of the heaven and as the sand which is on the seashore, and your descendants shall possess the gate of their enemies. In your seed all the nations of the earth shall be blessed, because you have obeyed My voice."[94]

"We already knew all that!" said the boy, slapping a palm on his forehead. "What is happening right now?"

"As we heard from the angel of the Lord," said the man, "Abraham was acting out of a fear of God. Perhaps God had doubt in Abraham's commitment to His will after his attempt to, well, 'pimp out' his wife again, as you put it. So here He swears to keep up His end of the deal once again. And here Abraham's words to his son, that God will provide a lamb, must be made good."

"That doesn't change the fact that this kid is traumatized for the rest of his life. Imagine, your first memory is of lying on a woodpile bound by rope, looking up at your senile father with a knife raised in the air, ready to plunge it into your belly when all of a sudden he looks skyward and starts talking to himself. 'What's that?' he says. 'You sure? It's no trouble at all, I'm already here. No, no, really, it would save me a load to carry on the way home.' Then he looks over at some poor goat caught in the bushes and slits its throat for no reason. Then all bloody and crazed he hoists you on his shoulders and says, 'Come on, kiddo. We're going home.' That could be a *very* confusing start to a young man's life."

"Let's not forget that, A, it's quite apparent Isaac is familiar with the tradition of sacrifice, as seen when he asks where the lamb is. And B, he puts up no fight when his father lays him upon the wood to be slain. Perhaps even in youth he can see the importance of sacrifice to the Almighty and can find honor and privilege in rising up to meet Him."

"Right. Which is why he needed to be bound," said the boy with rolling eyes.

"While I can see your point, I think you're missing the greater picture of the story."

"No, I think *you're* missing the greater picture of the story. This book is about traumatizing children, burning sons alive, sending bastards into the wild, sleeping with your drunken father. I mean, what kind of civilization do we descend from?"

"An *un*-civilization," said the man. "Which is exactly the point. We've fallen from paradise through sin. We're navigating the morals and ethics and learning how to live properly. Remember that no one walked before them to set a proper example. These were the beginning of times as a human race. Perhaps the Lord had to test the boundaries of rational thinking and reasoning in his chosen people, to see if they would go so far as to make a human sacrifice if they felt compelled."

"Clearly so," said the boy.

"Perhaps this is why it appears in Scripture, for future generations to learn from."

"Hmm," said the boy, scratching his chin. "I see what you did there."

"And let's not forget the most important thing," said the man, "which is C, Isaac is blessed with the experience of actually *see*ing the Lord for himself. That's an experience no man or child will so soon forget, and likely one that overwhelms any kind of trauma you're painting into our picture."

The boy had nothing to say to that, so the man continued with the story.

"At this point, Abraham returns to his young men and they all return to Beersheba. And to end the chapter we're told that Abraham learns the lineage of his family he left behind. The most important thing to note there is the introduction of Rebekah, the granddaughter of Abraham's brother, who is around Isaac's age. She'll become an important figure shortly."

"Noted," said the boy.

"In the next chapter, our beloved Sarah passes at the age of one hundred and twenty-seven. Abraham mourns her and asks the descendants of Heth, Canaan's second son, for a proper burial ground. They offer him the choicest land, the field of Ephron, which was said to have a cave. So Abraham lays Sarah to rest in the cave in the land of Canaan."

The boy took his water bottle and poured one out on the ground.

The old man bowed his head for a moment in return.

"Then, in the next chapter," said the man, "we return to the story of Isaac, beginning with mortality brought to the forefront of Abraham's mind by the death of his wife." The old man looked to his book and read:

> Now Abraham was old, well advanced in age, and the Lord had blessed Abraham in all things. So Abraham said to the oldest servant of his house, who ruled over all that he had, "Please, put your hand under my thigh, and I will make y—"[95]

"Stop," the boy raised his hand. "Stop. What's up with the thigh thing?"

"Well, Abraham is about to have his servant make a very serious oath. Here, listen," said the man:

> "...and I will make you swear by the Lord, the God of heaven and the God of the earth, that you will not take a wife for my son from the daughters of the Canaanites, among whom I dwell, but you shall go to my country and to my family, and take a wife for my son Isaac."[96]

"Abraham knows through prophecy that the Canaanites are destined for downfall, so he takes very seriously that his son should not marry one. Therefore he makes his trusted servant swear by God that he'll travel to his homeland and find Isaac a suitable wife."

"Yeah, I get the oath," said the boy, "but that doesn't answer my question."

"Well," said the man, fidgeting now, "this was a way of acknowledging the severity of the oath back then. In court today you place your hand upon the Bible and swear to tell the truth. It's something like that, but they didn't have the Bible then." He brought a fist to his lips and cleared his throat. "Shall we carry on?"

With slanting eyes, the boy said, "There's something you're not telling me."

"Well," said the man, fidgeting once again, "this, um, custom dates back to a different time, you see. In order to honor the symbol of the covenant with the Lord, 'thigh' has been considered a, well, euphemism." The man looked down at the page and began reading again:

And the servant sai—

"Stop," said the boy. "Stop. I'm still not following."

The man let out a heavy sigh. "The symbol of the covenant with God was th—"

"Whaaat?" The boy slapped his palm on his forehead again. "To make a promise they grabbed each other's cocks!?"

"'*And so* the servant said—'"

"What was wrong with a handshake?"

The man let out another sharp sigh and wiped a bit of sweat of his brow. "These were different *times*, my boy. Circumcision was the symbol of the holy covenant, and so in order to honor the Lord this was the gesture chosen to do so. Or perhaps 'under the thigh' was a reference to Abraham's, you know, promised *seed*."

"So he cupped his balls instead? That's even weirder!"

"Can we just carry on please?" said the man, glowing scarlet by now.

"This just keeps getting better and better," said the boy with a smile.

The man averted his eyes and carried on:

The servant said to him, "Suppose the woman is unwilling to follow me to this land? Should I have your son go back to the land you came from?"

Abraham answered him, "Make sure that you don't take my son back there. The Lord, the God of heaven, who took me from my father's house and from my native land, who spoke to me and swore to me, 'I will give this land to your offspring,' he will send his angel before you, and you can take a wife for my son from there. If the woman is unwilling to follow you, then you are free from this oath to me, but don't let my son go back there."[97]

The boy furrowed his brow. "And they're having this whole conversation while his hands are on his—"

"*Then* the servant puts his hand under Abraham's thigh," said the man:

...and swore to him concerning this matter. Then the servant took ten of his master's camels and departed, for all his master's goods were in his hand.[98]

"I see what they did there," said the boy.

The man rolled his eyes and read on:

And he arose and went to Mesopotamia, to the city of Nahor. And he made his camels kneel down outside the city by a well of water at evening time, the time when women go out to draw water.[99]

"Ahh," said the boy, "picking up chicks at the watering hole since three thousand BC."

The man shook his head and went on:

Then he said, "O Lord God of my master Abraham, please give me success this day, and show kindness to my master Abraham. Behold, here I stand by the well of water, and the daughters of the men of the city are coming out to draw water. Now let it be that the young woman to whom I say, 'Please let down your pitcher that I may drink,' and she says, 'Drink, and I will also give your camels a drink.' Let her be the one You have appointed for Your servant Isaac. And by this I will know that You have shown kindness to my master."

And it happened, before he had finished speaking, that behold, Rebekah, who was—[100]

"His cousin? Really? Of all the girls coming to the watering hole that night he picks his cousin?"

"Once removed," said the man. "The granddaughter of Abraham's brother, if you recall."

"Abraham made his servant cup his balls and promise to make his son marry his cousin? I'm not sure if this is better or worse than marrying your half sister."

"Matrimonial arrangements were made by the parents among pastoral tribes, my boy. The youth were not often married to strangers, but rather within the tribe."

When the boy said nothing, the man continued:

Now the young woman was very beautiful to behold, a virgin, no man had known her. And she went down to the well, filled her pitcher, and came up.

And the servant ran to meet her and said, "Please let me drink a little water from your pitcher."

So she said, "Drink, my lord." Then she quickly let her pitcher down to her hand and gave him a drink.[101]

"What the hell, man? Some dirty old vagabond comes sprinting at you in the dead of night screaming, 'Gimme your water,' and you're not even fazed? What a gal."

"Yes," said the man, "and when she finishes giving him a drink, she says, 'I will draw water for your camels also, until they have finished drinking.' Then she empties her pitcher into the trough and runs back to the well to draw once more water for his camels."

"She's gonna draw water for ten camels? But a camel can drink like thirty gallons at a time. That would take forever with that little pitcher she's got."

"Precisely," said the man. "What good nature! What courtesy! What humanity! And note, his servant doesn't park his camels outside a place of amusement or pleasure. He sought out a well, where a woman might come to fetch the water that provides for her family. There he asked the Lord for a clear sign of the woman he sought, and it was delivered before he could even finish speaking. When he asks only to drink a little water from her pitcher and she hastens to draw water for his camels as well, he sees the hospitable nature desired in a mother and wife for Isaac."

"Well it's certainly the most we've seen of a woman so far," said the boy.

The old man began to protest, but went on reading instead:

The man gazed at her in silence to learn whether the Lord had prospered his journey or not. When the camels had finished drinking, the man took a gold ring weighing a half shekel, and two bracelets for her arms weighing ten gold shekels, and said, "Please tell me whose daughter you are. Is there room in your father's house for us to spend the night?"[102]

"He gawks at her without saying anything before he pulls out a ring and says, 'Can I stay at your place?' Is she not creeped out by this?"

"We've seen the womanly qualities Abraham's servant was tasked to find, but the only thing that kept him in doubt was whether or not she was one of Abraham's kin. So he asks about her father and she replies here," said the man:

"I am the daughter of Bethuel, Milcah's son, whom she bore to Nahor." Again she said to him, "We have plenty of straw and feed, and room to stay overnight."

Then the man bowed low and worshiped the Lord. And he said, "Blessed be the Lord, the God of my master Abraham, who has not abandoned His kindness and His trustworthiness toward my master. As for me, the Lord has guided me in the way to the house of my master's brothers."[103]

The boy remained quietly listening, so the man went on.

"So Rebekah runs and tells her family what happened, and when her brother Laban sees the jewelry his sister has received from this stranger, he runs out to see him."

"To punch this creep in the face I hope," said the boy. "That or he's gonna rob him after ogling that jewelry."

"Not quite," said the man. "Instead, Laban says, 'Come in, O blessed of the Lord! Why do you stand outside? For I have prepared the house, and a place for the camels.' So Abraham's servant follows him to the house, and Laban unloads and feeds the camels and gives Abraham's men water to wash their feet."

"Might wanna wash those oath-taking hands as well," said the boy.

The man rolled his eyes. "Then food was served for them to eat, but Abraham's servant tells them, 'I will not eat until I have told about my errand.' And so he explains the mission he's on and tells the story of how this meeting with Rebekah came to be, concluding with the following," said the man:

> "I put the ring in her nose and the bracelets on her arms, and I bowed down and worshiped the Lord. I praised the Lord, the God of my master Abraham, who had led me on the right road to get the granddaughter of my master's brother for his son. Now if you will show kindness and faithfulness to my master, tell me. And if not, tell me, so I may know which way to turn."[104]

> Then Laban and Bethuel replied, "The matter has come from the Lord, so we cannot speak to you bad or good. Here is Rebekah before you, take her and go, and let her be the wife of your master's son, as the Lord has spoken."[105]

"Just like that, huh? Boy, people sure were trusting back then. Imagine if some guy bumped into your daughter at a grocery store and said he works for a rich man, and, 'Would you mind if I took her away. Oh, and cellphones don't work there so you'll have no communication whatsoever. And sorry but we'll have to be going now.'"

"Yes, these were times where the importance of marrying your daughter off to someone prominent was of great value to the family," said the man. "So when Abraham's servant hears this he bows to the Lord and brings gifts of jewelry and silver and gold to Rebekah's family. They eat and drink all night in celebration, and in the morning they set off on the journey back to Isaac with her family's blessing." The man paused to clear his throat before reading on:

> And Isaac went out to meditate in the field toward evening. And he lifted up his eyes and saw, and behold, there were camels coming.
>
> And Rebekah lifted up her eyes, and when she saw Isaac, she dismounted from the camel and said to the servant, "Who is that man, walking in the field to meet us?"
>
> The servant said, "It is my master." So she took her veil and covered herself.
>
> And the servant told Isaac all the things that he had done.
>
> Then Isaac brought her into the tent of Sarah his mother and took Rebekah, and she became his wife, and he loved her. So Isaac was comforted after his mother's death.[106]

The boy's face scrunched in disbelief. In a nerdy voice he said, "Here's where my mommy died. Will you comfort me by consummating our marriage on her bed?" Then he shook his head and said, "What a dreamboat. This is the weirdest story I've ever heard. I hope this is another one of your lessons on what *not* to do."

"I believe the repositioning of Sarah's funeral to Isaac's marriage is to show us that as one generation goes, another blossoms," said the man. "And moving Rebekah directly into the tent where the wife of the leader of the tribe formally dwelled is a symbol of her new place amongst who are soon to be Isaac's people."

"Uh-huh. And did you say Sarah was a hundred and twenty-seven when she died?"

"I did," said the man.

"So that would make Isaac, what, forty?"

Cautiously, the man said, "About, yes."

"No wonder his father was concerned. Isaac was following right in his footsteps living in his parent's basement till he was seventy. And did you say Rebekah was around the same age?"

Hesitant to see where this was going, the man said, "Mhm."

"So we've got a couple of forty-year-old cousin virgins, is what you're telling me."

With a sigh the man said, "Well we know Rebekah is a vir—"

"This story reminds me of a couple distant relatives that lived before the age of the internet," said the boy, smiling as he stared off into the trees. "They couldn't for the life of them figure out why they couldn't conceive." He restrained his laughter as he said, "For years they had trouble impregnating her colon." The boy looked back to find a grave look of concern on the old man's face. "Don't worry," he laughed, "they figured it out eventually. I just hope Abraham gave Isaac a lecture on the birds and the bees, or whatever they had back then."

"You have to take into account the context of the times," said the man. He was about to explain further but the boy raised his palm in the air.

"Just do me a favor."

"What is it?" said the man.

"Promise me, if I'm ever about to marry my cousin, you'll stop me."

"Sure," said the man.

"I don't care how hot she is," said the boy. "You promise?"

"I promise," said the man.

"Good," said the boy. Then he slowly stood and began to unzip his fly.

GENESIS 25-27

JACOB & ESAU

Who are you?
—Isaac

"Not all the days of even the Bible's greatest saints are re-markable," said the man. "Abraham lived to be one hundred and seventy-five without much more word of him before he was bur-ied in the same cave as Sarah."

The man watched the boy take a large swig of his water and place it down again. "*Ahhh.*"

The man shook his head with a smile. "Soon after, we hear of the children of Isaac and Rebekah, twins named Esau and Ja-cob. While Rebekah is pregnant, the Lord tells her, 'Two nations are in your womb, two peoples shall be separated from your body. One people shall be stronger than the other, and the older shall serve the younger.'"

The boy said, "Do I sense another Cain and Abel story com-ing?"

"We shall see," said the man, reading on:

When the boys grew up, Esau was a skillful hunter, a man of the field, while Jacob was a quiet man, dwelling in tents. Isaac loved Esau because he ate of his game, but Rebekah loved Jacob.[107]

Now Jacob cooked a stew, and Esau came in from the field, and he was weary. And Esau said to Jacob, "Please feed me with that same red stew, for I am weary."

But Jacob said, "Sell me your birthright as of this day."

And Esau said, "Look, I am about to die, so what is this birthright to me?"

Then Jacob said, "Swear to me as of this day."

So he swore to him, and sold his birthright to Jacob. And Jacob gave Esau bread and stew of lentils. Then he ate and drank, arose, and went his way. Thus Esau despised his birthright.[108]

"Can you explain the birthright thing?" said the boy "What's going on there?"

"Sure," said the man. "In those times, the firstborn was the rightful heir to the entire inheritance. I believe the rationale was that if you divide land and livestock amongst all your children, then everyone receives only a small parcel and a few goats. To avoid this, they gave nearly everything to the firstborn, which explains the rivalry between the twins. This tradition was arbitrary and unfair, but at least it was arbitrary and predictable."

"Jeez, what a rip-off."

"Precisely," said the man. "Which makes the selling of the birthright all the more significant. And the thoughtless manner in which Esau sells it for immediate gratification renders him unfit to be the heir. The words 'I am about to die' demonstrate his shortsightedness in that he will never live to inherit Canaan for himself, or any of the other supposed future blessings, so what use are they to him when he is dead and gone. But the manner in which Jacob takes advantage of his brother's frivolous attitude wasn't exactly commendable either."

"I would've done the same if that's all it took," said the boy. "If my options are to fool a fool or let his children inherit the land that mine could have instead, come on now, that's just Darwinism right there." The man chose not to comment as the boy smirked at him. "Anyway, what happens to Esau?"

"Well, it says when Esau is forty years old, he takes for wives Judith the daughter of Beeri the Hittite and Basemath the daughter of Elon the Hittite. Then it says they were a grief of mind to Isaac and Rebekah."

"Why were they a grief of mind?"

"As we saw with Abraham going to great lengths to find a suitable wife for Isaac, unions with these cursed people did not align with God's will."

With a wink the boy said, "For a second there I thought it was because there were two of them."

"That too, of course," said the man.

"Right, of course," said the boy. "Clear as day."

The man gave him a fleeting glare before he looked down to read again:

When Isaac was old and his eyes were dim so that he could not see, he called Esau his older son and said to him, "My son."

And he answered, "Here I am."

He said, "Behold, I am old. I do not know the day of my death. Now then, take your weapons, your quiver and your bow, and go out to the field and hunt game for me, and prepare for me delicious food, such as I love, and bring it to me so that I may eat, that my soul may bless you before I die."[109]

"Clearly he wasn't listening when the Lord said the elder should serve the younger."

"Actually, it's possible what the Lord shared with Rebekah about her pregnancy she kept to herself. If that were the case, then Isaac would have been acting according to tradition. But it's equally possible she shared this word from God with Isaac and he was trying to balance the injustice done to Esau by his brother. But you're right either way, that he was going against the Lord's will."

"Or maybe this is just what happens when parents pick favorites," said the boy.

The man nodded and read on:

But Rebekah overheard what Isaac had said to his son Esau. So when Esau left to hunt for the wild game, she said to her son Jacob, "Listen. I overheard your father say to Esau, 'Bring me some wild game and prepare me a delicious meal. Then I will bless you in the Lord's presence before I die.' Now, my son, listen to me. Do exactly as I tell you. Go out to the flocks, and bring me two fine young goats. I'll use them to prepare your father's favorite dish. Then take the food to your father so he can eat it and bless you before he dies."[110]

"Uh-oh," said the boy.

"Uh-oh is right. And Jacob recognizes that and tells his mother here," said the man:

> "But my brother Esau is a hairy man while I have smooth skin. What if my father touches me? I would appear to be tricking him and would bring down a curse on myself rather than a blessing."
>
> His mother said to him, "My son, let the curse fall on me. Just do what I say. Go and get them for me."
>
> So he went and got them and brought them to his mother, and she prepared some tasty food, just the way his father liked it.[111]

"That's right, let Mommy bear your burdens," said the boy. "You know, it really took no time at all for these chosen families to start manipulating each other."

"Manipulation as it was," said the man, "you have to wonder if we can excuse Rebekah's behavior, as her intention aligns with the divine prophecy."

"What a catch twenty-two that is," said the boy. "They really put a lot of importance on this blessing."

"The belief in birthrights and blessings was everything back then. And Rebekah knew this blessing was intended for Jacob, but she wrongs Isaac by deceiving him, she wrongs Jacob by tempting him to deceive, and she wrongs Esau by stealing from her own son. Here we see one of the first crooked measures used to further a divine purpose, as if the ends justify the means. This also gives Esau a reason to hate his brother, his family, and perhaps even his religion. But all were to blame for the circumstance this family found themselves in, not just her."

"So deep," said the boy, "so deep. But depending on how you look at it, Rebekah could be seen as a hero. She goes against her husband, shouldering a potential curse, and pushes Jacob to do what it takes in order to fulfill God's prophecy."

"What she did was certainly brave," said the man, reading on:

> Then Rebekah took the best garments of her elder son Esau, which were with her in the house, and put them on her younger son Jacob. And she put the skins of the young goats on his hands and on the smooth part of his neck. She also gave the delicious meal and the bread which she had made to her son Jacob.[112]

"Baby goat hair?"

"This may not be the sheep-like wool you're thinking of," said the man. "I believe it was more like camels' silky hair that resembled that of a human's." Then he read on:

> So he went in to his father and said, "My father."
>
> And he said, "Here I am. Who are you, my son?"
>
> Jacob said to his father, "I am Esau your firstborn. I have done just as you told me. Now sit up and eat of my game, that your soul may bless me."
>
> But Isaac said to his son, "How is it that you have found it so quickly, my son?"
>
> He answered, "Because the Lord your God granted me success."[113]

"Jeez. Bold move roping the Lord into this treachery."

"Bold indeed," said the man. "Then Isaac says to Jacob, 'Please come near, that I may feel you, my son, whether you are really my son Esau or not.'"

"You know, it really doesn't say much for their relationship that his father doubts him like that."

"Well, after he saw what a trick he played on his brother, can you blame him?"

"I guess not," said the boy. "So what happens?"

"So Jacob approaches his father and Isaac feels him and says, 'The voice is Jacob's voice, but the hands are the hands of Esau.' So he believes it's Esau and he blesses Jacob. But then he questions him again," said the man, reading further:

"Are you really my son Esau?"

He said, "I am."

He said, "Bring it near to me, and I will eat of my son's game, so that my soul may bless you."

So he brought it near to him, and he ate, and he brought him wine, and he drank.

Then his father Isaac said to him, "Come near now and kiss me, my son." And he came near and kissed him, and he smelled the smell of his clothing, and blessed him and said, "Surely, the smell of my son is like the smell of a field which the Lord has blessed. Therefore may God give you of the dew of heaven, of the fatness of the earth, and plenty of grain and wine. Let peoples serve you, and nations bow down to you. Be master over your brethren, and let your mother's sons bow down to you. Cursed be everyone who curses you, and blessed be those who bless you!"[114]

"Must be difficult for Jacob to bite his tongue during all this," said the boy.

"In what way?"

"Well, he's hearing this blessing that's supposed to belong to his only other sibling, not to mention his twin. Isaac says, 'Let your mother's sons bow down to you.'" The boy pretended to look around an empty room before he settled back on the man. "Well, I guess that means me."

"Huh," said the man, "I never noticed that."

"My twin is supposed to be my master now because he was born a second before me? Thanks for nothing, *Dad!*"

"It's a good point you raise."

"Anyway, keep going," said the boy.

So the man read on:

After Isaac finished blessing him, and Jacob had scarcely left his father's presence, his brother Esau came in from hunting. He too prepared some tasty food and brought it to his father. Then he said to him, 'My father, please sit up and eat some of my game, so that you may give me your blessing.'

His father Isaac asked him, "Who are you?"

"I am your son," he answered, "your firstborn, Esau."

Isaac trembled violently and said, "Who was it, then, that hunted game and brought it to me? I ate it just before you came and I blessed him, and indeed he will be blessed!"[115]

"Day late and a dollar short, pal," said the boy, as the man continued:

When Esau heard his father's words, he burst out with a loud and bitter cry and said to his father, "Bless me, bless me too, my father!"

But he said, "Your brother came deceitfully and took your blessing."[116]

Esau said, "Is he not rightly named Jacob? For he has cheated me these two times. He took away my birthright, and behold, now he has taken away my blessing." Then he said, "Have you not reserved a blessing for me?"

Isaac answered and said to Esau, "Behold, I have made him lord over you, and all his brothers I have given to him for servants, and with grain and wine I have sustained him. What then can I do for you, my son?"[117]

"Boy, they're taking this seriously. Can't Isaac just call Jacob back in and say, 'Hey, asshole, that wasn't very nice.' What's with the permanence of the blessing?"

"I don't have a good answer for you there," said the man. "All we can do is take from the story what we can. The fact of the matter is that he intended to give all the blessing he had to Esau because he loved him more, and not reserve a blessing for Jacob. But perhaps Isaac realizes what occurred here was the divine will of the Lord as originally intended. The blessing was not supposed to be a matter of subjective fatherly affection, but a right entrusted by the grace of God to the second born son."

"Alright, well let's hear what happens then."

So the man read on:

Esau said to his father, "Do you have only one blessing, my father? Bless me too, my father!" Then Esau wept aloud.

His father Isaac answered him, "Your dwelling will be away from the earth's richness, away from the dew of heaven above. You will live by the sword and you will serve your brother. But when you grow restless, you will throw his yoke from off your neck."[118]

"What does that mean?" said the boy. "Sounds intense."

"The metaphor is of a bull, yoked to pull a cart or plow. He's saying that when he gets tired of serving his brother he'll break free."

"Ah. That makes sense. Go on then," said the boy.

So the man read on:

Now Esau hated Jacob because of the blessing with which his father had blessed him, and he said to himself, "The days of mourning for my father are approaching, then I will kill my brother Jacob."

But the words of Esau her older son were told to Rebekah. So she sent an—[119]

"Wait a minute. If he said this to himself, how did she find out?"

"Well, obviously that's up to speculation based on the lack of detail," said the man. "Some have guessed Esau told his plan to a confidant or a friend and they warned Rebekah, while others have pushed for the idea that God warned Rebekah of Esau's idea."

"I guess it doesn't really matter," said the boy.

"It wouldn't affect the story either way," said the man, reading on:

> She sent for her younger son Jacob and said to him, "Your brother Esau is planning to avenge himself by killing you. Now then, my son, do what I say. Flee at once to my brother Laban in Harran. Stay with him for a while until your brother's fury subsides. When your brother is no longer angry with you and forgets what you did to him, I'll send word for you to come back from there. Why should I lose both of you in one day?"[120]

"Yeah," said the boy. "I'm sure he'll totally forget you stole his entire future in a few days. Who even remembers those kinds of things anyway."

"Keep that in mind as the story unfolds," said the man. "But did you notice the reflection of sibling rivalry with Cain and Abel here? "

"I did," said the boy, "but I'm having trouble sympathizing with Esau on this one. He kinda seems like a moron."

Smiling, the man read on:

> And Rebekah said to Isaac, "I am weary of my life because of the daughters of Heth. If Jacob takes a wife of the daughters of Heth, like these who are the daughters of the land, what good will my life be to me?"[121]

"What's that all about?" said the boy. "Seems kind of randomly thrown in there."

"The reason may be two-fold," said the man. "One, to obtain Isaac's consent to send Jacob to Laban, sparing him from any guilt regarding Esau's murderous intentions. And two, to conceal her involvement in the deception by presenting a concern of a proper wife for at least one of their sons."

"Ah, I see," said the boy. "More manipulation to throw him off the scent trail."

"Something like that," said the man.

GENESIS 28-31

JACOB & LABAN

Please give me some of your son's mandrakes.
—Rachel

"So Isaac tells Jacob to go to Haran to visit Rebekah's brother and instructs him to take a wife from his daughters. Then he blesses him before he goes."

"No scolding him for the deception, no slap on the wrist, nothing? Just gives him another blessing that he told Esau he didn't have."

"Afraid so," said the man, running his fingers over a few lines of text before reading on:

Now Jacob went out from Beersheba and went toward Hara—[122]

"What was that?" said the boy, stretching himself taller to peer at the text.

"Nothing important," said the man. "Just some minor details." But before he could finish speaking, the boy had reached for the book and turned it toward himself to read aloud:

> Esau saw that the daughters of Canaan did not please his father
> Isaac. So Esau went to Ishmael and took Mahalath the daughter
> of Ishmael, Abraham's son, the sister of Nebajoth, to be his wife
> in addition to the wives he had.[123]

The boy turned the book back toward the man and an awkward pause hung in the air as they stared at one other. "Minor details," said the boy.

"Well, Esau tries to align himself with his father's desire just to earn a blessing," said the man, "but he mends one fault by committing another when he had one too many wives as it was."

"I'm sure God will strike him down for this madness any day now," said the boy.

"Taking a third wife was certainly not God's will," said the man, "nor is taking another wife to gain your father's approval a good motivation. Esau is proving as reckless with his marital choices as was with the trading his birthright for stew."

"Look, I'm not saying Esau's the brightest bulb on the chandelier," said the boy, "but God isn't exactly coming down to drown anyone for taking multiple wives either. Unless there's an unknowing king getting duped, He seems to keep His nose out of everyone's marital business."

"If you're not convinced polygamy is troublesome yet, there are plenty more examples coming down the line. Anyway, Jacob leaves, and during his journey he arrives at a place to rest as the sun goes down. There he lays his head on a stone and dreams of a ladder that reaches to heaven from earth, with God's angels ascending and descending it:

There above it stood the Lord, and he said, "I am the Lord, the God of your father Abraham and the God of Isaac. I will give you and your descendants the land on which you are lying. Your descendants will be like the dust of the earth, and you will spread out to the west and to the east, to the north and to the south. All peoples on earth will be blessed through you and your offspring. I am with you and will watch over you wherever you go, and I will bring you back to this land. I will not leave you until I have done what I have promised you."[124]

"This is the first time Jacob hears from God, right?"

"That's right," said the man, "confirming that it's his descendants that will spread about the land."

"I wonder what Esau dreamed about that night," said the boy. "Probably more of that porridge."

The old man smiled before he read on:

Jacob awoke from his sleep and said, "Surely the Lord is in this place, and I did not know it." And he was afraid and said, "How awesome is this place! This is none other than the house of God, and this is the gate of heaven!" Then Jacob rose early in the morning, and took the stone that he had put at his head, set it up as a pillar, and poured oil on top of it.[125]

"Oil?"

"Oil was used as a symbol of an offering in those times," said the man. "Jacob didn't expect a manifestation of the Lord in a place so far from his father's home, so he is filled with awe when he finds himself at the gate of heaven. The pillar is the monument of the event, the pouring of oil an act of consecration to God."

The boy gave a nod and offered a palm toward the Bible, so the man continued:

> Then Jacob made a vow, saying, "If God will be with me and will watch over me on this journey I am taking and will give me food to eat and clothes to wear so that I return safely to my father's household, then the Lord will be my God and this stone that I have set up as a pillar will be God's house, and of all that You give me I will give You a tenth."[126]

"Ah. So this book was written by tax collectors," said the boy. "It's all making sense now."

"We'll see tithing mentioned again down the road, but here it's a form of gratitude for a safe journey and prosperity. And, as we see here, Jacob makes it safely to the land of the east. There, he finds himself at a well where sheepherders were gathering to water their flocks," said the man, looking down to read:

> And Jacob said to them, "My brothers, where are you from?"
> And they said, "We are from Haran."
> Then he said to them, "Do you know Laban the son of Nahor?"
> And they said, "We know him."
> So he said to them, "Is he well?"
> And they said, "He is well. And look, his daughter Rachel is coming with the sheep."[127]

"Couldn't have written it better myself," said the boy, as the man continued reading:

He said, "Behold, it is still high day, it is not time for the livestock to be gathered together. Water the sheep and go, pasture them."

But they said, "We cannot until all the flocks are gathered together and the stone is rolled from the mouth of the well, then we water the sheep."

While he was still speaking with them, Rachel came with her father's sheep, for she was a shepherdess. Now as soon as Jacob saw Rachel the daughter of Laban his mother's brother, and the sheep of Laban his mother's brother, Jacob came near and rolled the stone from the well's mouth and watered the flock of Laban his mother's brother.[128]

"Man," said the boy, "I really wish they'd clarify who Laban was."

"Yes, I'm not entirely sure the significance of the repetition," said the man, "but I believe it was written to emphasize what's unfolding here. First, at risk of inspiring the anger of the locals, this stranger disregards their tradition and removes the heavy stone himself. But apparently this display of personal strength was enough to keep them quiet."

"Why would he do that?"

"My guess is that he knew the story of Rebekah at the well and hoped to take after his mother by inspiring a similar feeling in Rachel. The repetition of 'Laban his mother's brother' might be to show his initial motivation was not inspired by some kind of lust over Rachel, but rather to honor his mother's desire. He was her favorite, after all, and surely wished to see her happy. Otherwise, you know, 'What good will my life be to me?'"

"Strange reason to find a wife," said the boy. "But what happens next?"

"Then Jacob kisses Rachel and he lifts up his voice and weeps."

"Just like that? Man, I gotta start hanging around more wells."

"Watering a flock of sheep is a work of time and labor," said the man. "Jacob volunteered no small service in aiding the young shepherdess. He was so overcome by joy in finding his kin so soon that he greeted her with affection before even sharing that he was the son of Rebekah."

"Yeah, but I mean some random crybaby walks up with puckered lips and you just go for it? Then *after* tongue wrestling he claims to be your cousin? These were definitely different times."

"This was done in a way of courtesy and civility, my boy. Likely a kiss on the cheek."

"Mhm," said the boy. "With that old I'm-a-fair-maiden-at-the-well routine? She's most definitely her aunty's niece."

The man rolled his eyes and read on:

Jacob told Rachel that he was a relative of her father and that he was Rebekah's son, and she ran and told her father. So when Laban heard the news about Jacob, his sister's son, he ran to meet him, and embraced him and kissed him, and brought him to his house. Then he told Laban all these things. And Laban said to him, "You certainly are my bone and my flesh." And he stayed with him a month.[129]

"Freeloader," said the boy.

"On the contrary," said the man. "We'll see Jacob offer his labor for free. But just remember, Jacob hasn't arrived with a plan. He's left his family to hide from his brother, and his uncle was kind enough to open his home, so it's only right he makes himself useful. But Laban says, 'Because you are my relative, should you therefore serve me for nothing? Tell me, what should your wages be?'"

"Alright, I take it back then," said the boy. "What were the wages?"

"Well, Laban had two daughters. The name of the elder was Leah, and the name of the younger was Rachel. We're told, 'Leah's eyes were delicate, but Rachel was beautiful of form and appearance.'"

"Is that a nice way of saying she was cross-eyed or something?"

The man stifled a laugh. "No, no. I believe this just means her eyes didn't sparkle with liveliness like Rachel's did. We see this line followed by 'but' to contrast Rachel's beauty in form and appearance, which seems to be a reference to both the shape of her body and look of her face in comparison."

The boy crossed his eyes and stuck out his tongue.

As the old man fought back a smile, he read:

Now Jacob loved Rachel, so he said, "I will serve you seven years for Rachel your younger daughter."[130]

"Seven *years*?" said the boy. "That's a prison sentence!"

"Keep in mind that wives had to be purchased back then, and Jacob brought no riches like Abraham's servant when seeking a wife for Isaac. All he had was his services to offer. You could say this was a labor of lo—"

"Oh stop it," said the boy. "Just keep reading."

The man smiled and read on:

> And Laban said, "It is better that I give her to you than that I should give her to another man. Stay with me."
>
> So Jacob served seven years for Rachel, and they seemed to him but a few days because of the love he had for her. Then Jacob said to Laban, "Give me my wife that I may go in to her, for my time is completed."[131]

"Seven years," said the boy. "Just think. Nowadays you only have to wait three dates, and you can even split the check." He winked, but the old man shook his head and read on:

> So Laban gathered together all the people of the place and made a feast.
>
> But in the evening he took his daughter Leah and brought her to Jacob, and he went in to her. And Laban gave his female servant Zilpah to his daughter Leah to be her servant. And in the morning, behold, it was Leah![132]

"Behold, it was Leah..? How dark was it?"

"Well, the Scripture doesn't exactly explain how Jacob could have done this without realizing. It's possible there was too much wine involved, or elaborate veils, or Jacob's wedding night jitters that caused him to miss this detail, but we'll never know for sure."

"Jitters?" said the boy. "Detail? You loved someone for seven years and you don't even..." He trailed off rubbing his temples. "Never mind. Just keep going."

So the man read:

> And Jacob said to Laban, "What is this you have done to me? Did I not serve with you for Rachel? Why then have you deceived me?"
>
> Laban said, "It is not so done in our country, to give the younger before the firstborn."[133]

"I mean, I guess he got what was coming to him after what he did to Esau," said the boy. "But Laban and Rebekah were certainly cut from the same cloth, huh? Maybe Leah was a better match for Jacob anyway if she was willing to go along with this trickery."

"Maybe so," said the man, reading Laban's next line:

> "Complete the week of this one, and we will give you the other also in return for serving me another seven years."
>
> Jacob did so, and completed her week. Then Laban gave him his daughter Rachel to be his wife. And Laban gave his female servant Bilhah to his daughter Rachel to be her servant. So Jacob went in to Rachel also, and he loved Rachel more than Leah, and served Laban for another seven years.[134]

"*Fourteen* years he's gonna work for this girl? Man, they don't make 'em like they used to."

"We have to wonder if Jacob's plan was to work for seven years and then return home to with his beloved wife Rachel. If so, that dream came to an end when he became legally bound to Leah by the kind of deception he once practiced himself. And Laban's excuse about tradition is more of an insult than anything," said the man, "but it was an even more powerful lesson to Jacob when he's reminded of cheating his older brother."

"What a karmic slap in the face that was," said the boy.

"He could have refused to marry Rachel and left, or refused to marry Leah and ruined his chance with Rachel, or he could have demanded Rachel and told Laban he wasn't going to be cheated and face the consequences. But instead, Laban seems to know Jacob would continue serving him in order to marry Rachel as well."

"Tough choices," said the boy. "And so?"

"So we learn that 'when the Lord saw that Leah was unloved, He opened her womb, but Rachel was barren.'"

"Of course..." said the boy, rolling his eyes as the man continued:

So Leah conceived and bore a son, and she called his name Reuben, for she said, "The Lord has surely looked on my affliction. Now therefore, my husband will love me."

Then she conceived again and bore a son, and said, "Because the Lord has heard that I am unloved, He has therefore given me this son also." And she called his name Simeon.

She conceived again and bore a son, and said, "Now this time my husband will become attached to me, because I have borne him three sons." Therefore his name was called Levi.

And she conceived again and bore a son, and said, "Now I will praise the Lord." Therefore she called his name Judah. Then she stopped bearing.[135]

"Wow. That's messed up. Rachel's infertile while her manipulative sister is knocked up by her drunkenly blind lover?"

"It gets worse," said the man.

"Lay it on me," said the boy.

"When Rachel bears Jacob no children, she envies her sister and says to Jacob, 'Give me children, or else I die!'"

"She sounds like Esau."

"How so?"

"Well, the first thing we hear from each of them is, 'Give me something or I'll die.'"

The man smiled. "You know, I never made that connection, but you're right. Often the first line of a biblical character's speech is a defining quality of who they are."

"I'll keep an eye out for that," said the boy.

The man gave a nod as he read on:

And Jacob's anger was aroused against Rachel, and he said, "Am I in the place of God, who has withheld from you the fruit of the womb?"

So she said, "Here is my maid Bilhah. Go in to her, and she will bear a child on my knees, that I also may have children by her." Then she gave him Bilhah her maid as wife, and Jacob went in to her. And Bilhah conceived and bore Jacob a son.[136]

"Don't these people learn anything?" said the boy. "This is what happens when you stay in the family. Stories repeat themselves."

"In contrast, though, when Sarah has a child through Hagar, she immediately regrets it. Rachel, on the other hand, receives the baby born to Bilhah as a gift from God. Here, listen," said the man:

Then Rachel said, "God has judged my case, and He has also heard my voice and given me a son." Therefore she called his name Dan.

And Rachel's maid Bilhah conceived again and bore Jacob a second son. Then Rachel said, "With great wrestlings I have wrestled with my sister, and indeed I have prevailed." So she called his name Naphtali.[137]

"Is she delusional?"

"It's not precisely clear what this second child means for Rachel in prevailing over her sister. Perhaps it's a reference to where Leah has stopped bearing and Rachel is now the one producing sons."

"But they're not even her kids."

"Well, in the context of the times, with the idea of surrogate mothers, they belong to her. Or at least that's how she justifies it in her mind. But it's not exactly an honorable victory either way. She says this in the spirit of weaning her husband's affection off the already unloved Leah even more, boasting victory in some kind of child-bearing war."

"Not exactly a healthy motivation for having children," said the boy.

"No," said the man, "not at all. And had Rachel's heart not been influenced by bitter motivations, she may have seen her sister's children as near to her, instead of some kind of adversarial army being birthed against her. But children whom she had the right to claim as her own were more desirable than finding reasons to love her nephews. She even took pleasure in naming them as symbols of rivalry, Dan meaning something like 'judgment,' as God offered her vindication, and Naphtali something akin to 'struggle,' used to express this idea of overcoming this wrestling match she perceives."

"Let's see how this birth war plays out then," said the boy.

With a nod the man read:

When Leah saw that she had stopped bearing, she took Zilpah her maid and gave her to Jacob as wife. And Leah's maid Zilpah bore Jacob a son. Then Leah said, "What good fortune!" So she called his name Gad.

And Leah's maid Zilpah bore Jacob a second son. Then Leah said, "I am happy, for the daughters will call me blessed." So she called his name Asher.

Now Reuben went in the days of wheat harvest and found mandrakes in the field, and brought them to his mother Leah. Then

Rachel said to Leah, "Please give me some of your son's mandrakes."[138]

"What are mandrakes?"

"Mandrakes are a plant with roots like a potato, but they fork
and resemble a human body with open legs." The boy's eyebrows shot upward. "Precisely," said the man. "They were believed to be an aphrodisiac and something of a fertility drug back
then."

"No wonder she wants them."

"That's right," said the man, looking down at the Bible
again:

> But she said to her, "Is it a small matter that you have taken away
> my husband? Would you take away my son's mandrakes also?"
>
> And Rachel said, "Therefore he will lie with you tonight for your
> son's mandrakes."[139]

"Poor Jacob, getting passed around between all his wives
and concubines."

"Yes, we don't hear much protest from Jacob in these matters. But there is some indication he hasn't been spending much
time with Leah as of late, based on the bitter dialogue anyway.
And notice the parallels between these sisters and Jacob and his
brother," said the man, "a rivalry where one sibling barters a
privilege for food."

"Right," said the boy, "reversed for the older and younger
this time."

"Good catch," said the man, reading on again:

When Jacob came out of the field in the evening, Leah went out to meet him and said, "You must come in to me, for I have surely hired you with my son's mandrakes." And he lay with her that night.[140]

"Jeez, she has to hire her own husband to knock her up again? But didn't it just say she stopped bearing children?"

"Perhaps Jacob's love for Rachel was the overwhelming force that kept him out of Leah's bedchamber, but it's also possible the reason Leah stopped bearing is because Rachel began controlling Jacob. How, we don't exactly know. Perhaps the 'else I die' was a threat of suicide, or perhaps there was some other way of influencing his behavior. Either way, it's apparent Leah was still fertile once Rachel allowed Jacob to spend the night with her as a bargaining chip for her own chance at fertility."

"Taking it back to the garden with that one," said the boy. The man scrunched his brow in confusion, so the boy clarified. "Well, when God was punishing Eve, didn't He say her desire would be to control her husband?"

The man looked up and to the left for a moment. Then he marked the page he was on with his tassel and flipped back in the text. He scanned the chapter until he found the line:

"Your desire shall be for your husband, and he shall rule over you."[141]

The boy smiled. "Am I wrong?"

Narrowing his eyes, the man said, "It appears so."

"Maybe out of context," said the boy, "or with that particular translation, but it was said in the same manner in which God warns Cain about sin crouching at the door."

The man ran his finger down the next page until he found the line:

"Its desire is for you, but you must rule over it."[142]

"Right," said the boy. "Eve's desire to influence her husband and eat the fruit of the tree led to the punishment of pain in childbearing. Rachel's desires to control her husband and take things into her own hands with mandrakes led to the punishment of infertility."

"But I think we established Adam's silence in convincing Eve to stick with the divine command was equally to blame," said the man.

"And here Jacob's following in Adam's silent footsteps," said the boy. "All I'm pointing out is that God established wives should be governed by their husbands and no one is listening or speaking up about it, creating headaches all around." A smirk grew across the boy's face as he finished speaking.

The man tried to maintain a skeptical furrow of his brow, but his reaction melted into a smile. "I'm not sure about the accuracy of what you're saying, but it's certainly a clever parallel,

I'll give you that much. Though this raises the question of why Rachel would have been infertile *before* all this happened."

"Maybe it's like with Cain," said the boy, "where God recognized jealousy inside of him so He put him through a test to bring it to the surface."

The man turned his head sideways to stare at the boy through the corner of his eye. "You know, you're smarter than you look."

The boy laughed. "What's that supposed to mean?"

The man smiled as he flipped back to his tasseled page. "Oh nothing."

"What question this really raises," said the boy, "is if God frowns upon polygamy, why didn't he nip this whole thing in the bud before it started?"

The man raised an eyebrow. "And how should He have done that, oh wise one?"

"How about, oh, I don't know, any way He pleases? He came to Abimelech in a dream, He set plagues upon Pharaoh, He could have drown someone in another spell of rain. Why the sudden silence in the matter of two wives? Not to mention *sisters*."

"Are you not seeing the trouble that comes from having siblings as wives?" said the man. "There are lessons to be learned from these stories. Perhaps that was God's plan all along, to show us the troubles these situations come with."

"See, I don't know if that argument holds water. A little bickering is natural in any relationship. If anything, these are lessons on how to manage more than one. At this point I think God recognizes polygamy as a natural evolution in His creation. He's holding his mighty tongue just to see how it all plays out. If He was dead set against it, He would have come down and spoken to Laban, saying, 'Don't you trick the chosen one with your deception!' *Or*, if the goal was really to teach a lesson, after karma came back around and bit Jacob, when he tried to take a second wife God could have wagged his finger and said, 'Ah, ah, ah. Only one wife allowed. Maybe now you'll think twice about deceiving family!' Now *that's* a story with a lesson."

"I don't think God would be so cruel as to deny His chosen one true love. I think laboring for another seven years is punishment enough," said the man. "Besides, if God had to interject every time He didn't like something, His children would never learn for themselves."

"Exactly," said the boy. "He only chooses to interfere on the most offensive accounts. Like when the sons of God were mingling with the daughters of men, or when man stayed in one place building a tower instead of subduing the earth, or when a prophet started lying to pimp out his wife for economic gain. He never interferes in man's personal relationships by imposing some divine law. He lets us figure it out and learn what's best for ourselves."

"I don't know if I care for the way you're twisting these stories to fit your narrative," said the man. "This goes against traditional understanding."

"Fine," said the boy. "Agree to disagree. Let's move on."

Without saying anything more, the man read on:

God listened to Leah, and she conceived and bore Jacob a fifth son. Leah said, "God has given me my wages, because I have given my maid to my husband." Then Leah said, "God has rewarded me for giving my servant to my husband." So she named him Issachar.[143]

"How weird," said the boy. "God rewards her for sharing her husband."

The old man ignored him with an eye roll and kept reading:

Leah conceived again and bore Jacob a sixth son. Then Leah said, "God has presented me with a precious gift. This time my husband will treat me with honor, because I have borne him six sons." So she named him Zebulun

Some time later she gave birth to a daughter and named her Dinah.[144]

"Just an insignificant afterthought," said the boy. "Hardly worth mentioning."

"The Scripture is often short on details," said the man, "even pertaining to genealogies. There may have been many more children in this family, boys or girls, but the ones mentioned go on to become characters in later stories, making their mention necessary, Dinah included."

"Fair enough," said the boy, so the man read the next line:

Then God remembered Rachel, and God listened to her and opened her womb.[145]

"God sure seems to forget his chosen people a lot," said the boy. "We still don't know what she did that deserves punishment anyway."

"I won't pretend to know God's motivations," said the man, "but a major theme of this chapter is around who gives the gift of children, and that is God and God alone. No personal scheme or mandrake will work to skirt around His almighty plans. Perhaps this was all a lesson to humble Rachel and correct her bad-tempered nature and trust in 'fertility potatoes,' as you put it, over His will."

The boy nodded, so the man read on:

So she conceived and gave birth to a son, and said, "God has taken away my disgrace."

And she named him Joseph, saying, "May the Lord give me another son."

Now it came about, when Rachel had given birth to Joseph, that Jacob said to Laban, "Send me away, so that I may go to my own place and to my own country. Give me my wives and my children for whom I have served you, and let me go, for you yourself know my service which I have rendered you."[146]

"I see Jacob's finally growing a spine," said the boy. "He's been mostly a pushover so far."

"Yes," said the man, "his demand implies that Laban is still the head of the family, possessing control over his daughters and their children. Jacob's guess is that Laban will not willingly lose his labor, or proximity to his daughters and grandchildren, but he also knows Laban can be deceiving when it comes to the terms of their agreement. But we see there is perhaps a shift in the dynamic when Laban says, 'Please stay, if I have found favor in your eyes, for I have learned by experience that the Lord has blessed me for your sake.' Then he tells Jacob to name his wages and he will give them."

"That's crafty," said the boy. "First Laban butters him up knowing Jacob will lead with a modest proposal. Then he can counter with an even lower offer if he wants to."

"Greedy men will mold their words to serve themselves," said the man. "And although Laban admits he's prospered from Jacob's company, he presents his refusal to let Jacob go as an opportunity. He wants him to agree to a new deal since he's fulfilled the terms of the old one."

"Which is slippery territory for Jacob," said the boy, "considering Laban is prone to trickery."

The old man agreed with a nod before reading on:

Jacob said to him, "You know how I have worked for you and how your livestock has fared under my care. The little you had before I came has increased greatly, and the Lord has blessed you wherever I have been. But now, when may I do something for my own household?"[147]

He said, "What shall I give you?"

Jacob said, "You shall not give me anything. If you will do this for me, I will again pasture your flock and keep it. Let me pass through all your flock today, removing from it every speckled and spotted sheep and every black lamb, and the spotted and speckled among the goats, and they shall be my wages. So my honesty will answer for me later, when you come to look into my wages with you. Every one that is not speckled and spotted among the goats and black among the lambs, if found with me, shall be counted stolen."[148]

"Alright, what's that all about?"

"Laban asks, 'What do you want from me?' and Jacob surprises him by saying, 'Nothing right now, but if I continue to tend your flock I want some of your livestock as payment,' which was a common exchange for shepherds back then. Normally it was something like twenty percent of the flock, but Jacob asks only for the black and speckled sheep and white and spotted goats, which seems like a nominal fee considering these were rare among the primarily white sheep and black goats of the East in those times."

"Hmm," said the boy. "Seems like he's up to something."

"Perhaps, but of course the deal seems agreeable to Laban," said the man, "so he accepts. But to further ensure this one-sided deal, Laban separates all the mixed-colored animals from the pure-coated ones so there is no chance they'll crossbreed and multiply."

"I have a feeling karma is coming around," said the boy.

The man smiled and read on:

Jacob then took branches of fresh poplar, almond, and plane wood, and peeled the bark, exposing white stripes on the branches. He set the peeled branches in the troughs in front of the sheep in the water channels where the sheep came to drink.

And the sheep bred when they came to drink. The flocks bred in front of the branches and bore streaked, speckled, and spotted young. Jacob separated the lambs and made the flocks face the streaked sheep and the completely dark sheep in Laban's flocks. Then he set his own stock apart and didn't put them with Laban's sheep.

Whenever the stronger of the flock were breeding, Jacob placed the branches in the troughs, in full view of the flocks, and they would breed in front of the branches. As for the weaklings of the flocks, he did not put out the branches. So it turned out that the weak sheep belonged to Laban and the stronger ones to Jacob. And the man became very rich. He had many flocks, female and male slaves, and camels and donkeys.[149]

"He put sticks in the water and it magically changed their fur? Help me out here."

"It's something like, he's learned over the years that what the dams perceive while in heat can influence the patterns on their young after the rut. In any case, they bore many more streaked and spotted animals than plainly colored ones."

"I'll give you a pass on that one," said the boy. "What's next?"

"Next, Jacob overhears Laban's sons talking about him," said the man, reading on:

"Jacob has taken all that was our father's and has built this wealth from what belonged to our father." And Jacob saw from Laban's face that his attitude toward him was not the same as before.

The Lord said to him, "Go back to the land of your ancestors and to your family, and I will be with you."[150]

"Oh, there you are, God. Fourteen years later."

"Twenty," said the man.

"*Twenty*?" said the boy. "Wouldn't that make him, what, like ninety when he had to move back to his parents' basement with the gals?"

"Something like that," said the man. "So Jacob fills in Rachel and Leah on what's happened, informing them about the deal he made with their father. He tells them how in a dream he saw it was God's doing that only the spotted and speckled rams were breeding among the sheep, that God has taken the livestock from their father and given them to him because of the way Laban had been treating him." The man looked down to read:

Rachel and Leah said to him, "Do we still have any share or inheritance in our father's house? Are we not regarded by him as foreigners? For he has sold us, and has also entirely consumed our purchase price. Surely all the wealth which God has taken away from our father belongs to us and our children. Now then, do whatever God has told you."[151]

"Oh how a common enemy unites us," said the boy.

"Precisely," said the man.

GENESIS 32-33

JACOB RETURNS

Your name shall no longer be called Jacob,
but Israel, for you have struggled with God
and with men, and have prevailed.
—Unknown

"So Jacob went on his way and sent messengers before him to find Esau," said the man:

He instructed them, "This is what you are to say to my lord Esau. 'Your servant Jacob says, I have been staying with Laban and have remained there till now. I have cattle and donkeys, sheep and goats, male and female servants. Now I am sending this message to my lord, that I may find favor in your eyes.'"

When the messengers returned to Jacob, they said, "We went to your brother Esau, and now he is coming to meet you, and four hundred men are with him."[152]

"This number four hundred," said the man, "carries a militaristic connotation in ancient Hebrew, so Jacob becomes rightly afraid and divides his people and flocks into two companies."

"Up to some trickery again, no doubt," said the boy.

"Well, his message to Esau was cordial and apologetic," said the man, "so it seems to have come from a place of maturity."

"Or cowardice."

"Or fear, yes," said the man. "He didn't exactly leave on the best terms with his brother, but he does call Esau 'my lord,' so we can see it is out of respect, not conflict, that he informs him of his arrival. He also lists that which he can offer in order to find favor in his brother's eyes. But there is certainly fear, as we'll see."

"Clearly Esau doesn't like that he's acquired so much wealth if he's sent an army to greet him," said the boy. "Seems like jealousy over that blessing has been brewing for the last twenty years."

"And who can blame him?" said the man. "So anyway, Jacob's idea is that if Esau attacks one company, the other can still escape. So he prays to the Lord to deliver him from the hand of his brother for fear that Esau will attack his children and their mothers. Then he makes camp for the night and gathers an offering for his brother that consists of 'two hundred female goats and twenty male goats, two hundred ewes and twenty rams, thirty milk camels with their colts, forty cows and ten bulls, twenty female donkeys and ten foals.'"

"That's a lot of animals."

"Yes, this was no small gift back then either," said the man. "Livestock provided a renewable source of milk, meat, labor, and clothing. The size of this gift wasn't just a token of kindness. Jacob was giving his brother a large portion of his wealth."

"And how does it go over?"

"Well, Jacob assigns servants to each of these different herds and sends them ahead one by one with space in between, instructing each to tell Esau, 'They are your servant Jacob's. It is a present sent to my lord Esau, and behold, he also is behind us.'"

"He doesn't even have the balls to meet him head-on? Just sends his servants ahead for slaughter? Boy, if his wives weren't barren before, their wombs are certainly dried up now."

"I'm not so sure I'd have the courage to ride to my doom either," said the man. "To send a train of gifts with the intention of gradually wearing down Esau's wrath seems pretty clever. Increasing the emotional impact of each additional gift is another example of Jacob's mastery of manipulation."

"He always was a thinking man," said the boy. "So, does it work?"

"Well," said the man, "before we get to that, we have what is possibly the strangest verse in all of Genesis."

"Stranger than a talking snake and impossible flood?"

"I'll let you decide," said the man. "Jacob wanders away from his camp, and then here it says he 'was left alone, and a man wrestled with him until the breaking of day.'"

"A random man?" said the boy. "Just appears out of nowhere and *wrestles* him? For hours longer than an Olympic wrestler could endure? You're right. That is strange."

"That's not even the strangest part," said the man. "But keep in mind this theme of wrestling that has occurred throughout this story so far. Esau and Jacob, Jacob and Laban, Leah and Rachel. Here the imagery becomes literal in this important moment."

"Alright," said the boy, "let's hear it then."

"When the man sees that he cannot overpower Jacob, he touches the socket of Jacob's hip, and his hip goes out of joint. But then the man says, 'Let me go, for the day breaks.'"

"What is he, a vampire or something?"

"That's the thing," says the man. "Some people interpret this man as God, or one of God's angels. But why this unease about daybreak? God and His angels have appeared in daylight before, so this may contradict that theory."

"Unless God had a dentist appointment He was late for," said the boy.

"Very good," the man laughed. "Perhaps that's the reason."

"Well, obviously it's some kind of spiritual... *thing*," said the boy, "if he can dislocate a hip with a measly touch."

"Yes, it's very unclear," said the man. "So anyway, Jacob recognizes this man has this kind of supernatural power, so he says, 'I will not let you go unless you bless me!' So the man asks, 'What is your name?' Which, again, couldn't be our omniscient God, who has the habit of calling his chosen people by name. But either wa—"

"Hold on a sec," said the boy. "You told me God asked where Adam was in the garden to give Adam a chance to repent, even though God already knew where he was."

The man paused and looked off into nowhere. "Good point."

"You said Jacob means 'supplanter,' right?"

"Yes, often understood to mean one who circumvents or usurps."

"Right. So maybe this is God giving Jacob a chance to repent somehow, because the last time someone asked Jacob for his name he said it was Esau."

The old man's eyes lit up. "My boy, you may be on to something there. Because in the next line Jacob tells the man his name and the man says, 'Your name shall no longer be called Jacob, but Israel, for you have struggled with God and with men, and have prevailed.'"

"Right there," said the boy. "He just said you've struggled with God."

"Well, he *refers* to God, but he doesn't say, 'You have struggled with Me, God.' And he also says you have struggled with men, so I never thought it was clear enough to assume this was God. Perhaps a dream of the spirit of Esau, or an externalization of all that Jacob had to contend with leading up to this reunion."

"But we haven't seen any other kind of spiritual beings at this point," said the boy, "besides God or His angels."

"But that doesn't mean there's no room for a first either," said the man. "But whoever this figure is, this victory results in a name change, perhaps symbolizing that a metaphorical debt has been paid, that God's good grace has been restored, instead of having to seize more blessings through devious schemes."

"Well," said the boy, "maybe it was a drunk night owl with a light sensitivity, wandering through a field looking for a fight and getting lucky with a pressure point."

"I'd have trouble believing that one," said the man, "but we can certainly throw it into the hat of theories anyway."

"Maybe we shouldn't," said the boy. "I think if the whole nation of Israel was named because some bum said so it might take away the magic."

"Out of the hat it goes then," said the man. "In any case, Jacob says, 'Tell me your name, I pray,' and the man says, 'Why is it that you ask about my name?' So whomever or whatever it was resists recognition. He does, however, bless Jacob before he goes. Then Jacob calls the name of the place Peniel, 'For I have seen God face to face, and my life is preserved.' And just as he crosses over Peniel back to camp, the sun rises as he limps on his hip."

"I mean that seems pretty clear," said the boy, "at least in his eyes."

"In light of what you've just shown me, I might have to agree with you."

"Come on, man, this is your book. *I* have to convince *you* that it's God? What kind of believer are you?"

"Well," the old man chuckled, "I guess I was feeling tied to my old ways of thinking, but I think that can change."

"Better than a drunk bum," said the boy.

"Better than a drunk bum," said the man.

"And so?"

"And so 'Jacob lifted his eyes—'"

"I thought you said he was Israel now."

"Well yes," said the man, "but the name change doesn't appear fulfilled in the same way Abram was henceforth known as Abraham. The Scripture still refers to Jacob by his birth name at times. I'm not sure why, to be honest. Perhaps Israel is more of a synonym in this case, or the change was more of a symbol of internal changes."

"Just one more of those things we'll never have an answer to I guess," said the boy.

"That's right," said the man, reading on again:

Then Jacob looked up and saw Esau coming with his four hundred men. So he divided the children among Leah, Rachel, and his two servant wives. He put the servant wives and their children at the front, Leah and her children next, and Rachel and Joseph last.[153]

"So we've learned nothing about playing favorites," said the boy.

"Indeed, Jacob's motivations aren't outright stated, but I think you've got a pretty firm grasp on the reason for the ordering. It may seem harsh that his most beloved family will have the best chance at escape if Esau attacks, but probably not an uncommon attitude in that era either."

"I'm imagining all of Joseph's brothers craning their necks to look at the back of the line at the favorite son," said the boy.

"Indeed, this is perhaps where the resentment starts brewing that we'll see later on, but fortunately we don't have to witness any kind of violence here. Jacob approaches his brother before them and bows down seven times. Esau then runs to meet him, and they embrace and begin to weep upon each other's shoulders."

"Oh how the blessing tables have turned," said the boy. "Look who's bowing down to who now. But I guess all those gifts softened up Esau after all, huh?"

"Yes, then he lifts his eyes and inquires about all the women and children," said the man, reading on:

"Who are these with you?"

Jacob said, "The children whom God has graciously given your servant."

Then the servants drew near, they and their children, and bowed down. Leah likewise and her children drew near and bowed down. And last Joseph and Rachel drew near, and they bowed down.

184

Esau said, "What do you mean by all this company that I met?"

Jacob answered, "To find favor in the sight of my lord."

But Esau said, "I have enough, my brother. Keep what you have for yourself."

Jacob said, "No, please, if I have found favor in your sight, then accept my present from my hand. For I have seen your face, which is like seeing the face of God, and you have accepted me. Please accept my blessing that is brought to you, because God has dealt graciously with me, and because I have enough."

Thus he urged him, and he took it.[154]

"Better that way," said the boy. "There's probably a small part of Esau that still resents what happened. Something of a formal apology might discourage that part of him bubbling up later on."

"Precisely," said the man. "A gift of this size was substantial enough to erase the loss of a birthright, at least in material terms. But 'I have seen your face, which is like seeing the face of God' is also a very flattering statement for Esau. Jacob equates the judgment of his brother with that of the highest of virtues, something that implies his recognition of a larger principle at stake, one which is vital to reconcile as they set an example in front of their family as well as hundreds of men that dwell in their lands."

"Powerful," said the boy.

"Indeed," said the man. "Then Esau offers to escort Jacob's caravan along their journey, but Jacob politely declines, informing his brother that they could not keep up the pace of his men with his nursing sheep and tired children. And so they go their separate ways."

"Ahh, and all is right in world," said the boy. "But just to sum up this chapter, for clarity's sake and all, God punishes Esau for taking three wives by making him the leader of a nation with so much wealth that he was in a position to turn down a birth right's worth of livestock from his brother, God's polygamous chosen one whom Israel is named after, who was blessed with that much wealth to spare himself, all because God hates polygamy. Am I getting this right?"

With frustration boiling to the surface the man said, "In case you're not listening, these stories of polygamy have been examples of 'show don't tell' when it comes to the headaches of marriage beyond just a man and a woman."

"Yeah, but point to a *monogamous* marriage that's gone well so far," said the boy. "Eve dragged her husband out of paradise by tempting him to sin. Rebekah tricked her blind husband into giving her favorite son the blessing. Who else are we supposed to look to? Laban, who sold his daughters into polygamy? Lot, who had sex with both his daughters after his wife turned into a salt pillar? There are no good examples to follow."

"Well Noah's family was clearly on the right path," said the man, "while the sons of God were busy fornicating with the daughters of men. But I'd like to know where this idea that you need multiple wives to be happy is coming from?"

"No one's saying that," said the boy. "I'm just trying to point out that there's no divine rule against different kinds of relationships, except for your own ideal painted onto these stories. We've heard nothing from God in this regard."

"We're still in the early days, my boy. There are plenty of laws and examples coming."

"And I'll be patiently waiting," said the boy. "But until then, God and I would appreciate it if you stopped putting words in His mouth."

There was a strong pause where they both held a straight face, but after fighting back smiles, they each burst into laughter.

GENESIS 34-36

SIMEON, LEVI, & REUBEN

But on this condition we will consent to you.
—Sons of Jacob

"The next chapter begins with Dinah, Jacob's daughter with Leah," said the man:

> [She] went out to see the daughters of the land. And when Shechem the son of Hamor the Hivite, prince of the country, saw her, he took her and lay with her, and violated her. His soul was strongly attracted to Dinah the daughter of Jacob, and he loved the young woman and spoke kindly to the young woman.[155]

"Huh? He rolls over and says, 'So how was that rape for you, sweetie?' What does that even mean?"

"This is certainly one of the more bizarre scenes in Genesis," said the man. "An already tragic event, one often inspired by hatred or lust, takes an unexpected turn when Shechem has the audacity to advance with romantic words when his soul is drawn to Dinah. The scene becomes even stranger when Shechem insists to his father, 'Get me this young woman as a wife.'"

"Wow," said the boy. "What a little pr—"

"*Prince*," said the man. "An extraordinarily entitled little prince. With an extreme lack of self-control, as we'll see when he blindly agrees to do anything to get his wish. But before we get ahead of ourselves, Jacob hears of this and maintains his composure until his sons come in from tending livestock in the field. That's when Shechem and Hamor speak with Jacob about arranging a marriage and they all learn of what's happened. As you can imagine, Jacob's sons become very angry when they hear what's been done to their sister."

"No kidding," said the boy.

"Yes, but Hamor tells them the following," said the man:

"The soul of my son Shechem longs for your daughter. Please give her to him to be his wife. Make marriages with us. Give your daughters to us, and take our daughters for yourselves. You shall dwell with us, and the land shall be open to you. Dwell and trade in it, and get property in it."[156]

"I guess the tree didn't grow very far from the apple," said the boy.

"Not far at all. And then Shechem chimes in here," said the man:

"Let me find favor in your eyes, and I will give you whatever you ask. Make the price for the bride and the gift I am to bring as great as you like, and I'll pay whatever you ask me. Only give me the young woman as my wife."[157]

"Sounds like he's trying to bribe his way out of justice at this point," said the boy.

"Yes, well, the sons of Jacob see another problem," said the man, reading on:

> "We cannot do this thing, to give our sister to one who is uncircumcised, for that would be a disgrace to us. Only on this condition will we agree with you—that you will become as we are by every male among you being circumcised. Then we will give our daughters to you, and we will take your daughters to ourselves, and we will dwell with you and become one people. But if you will not listen to us and be circumcised, then we will take our daughter, and we will be gone."[158]

"And this pleases Hamor and Shechem," said the man, "enough so that they don't hesitate to comply."

"What are the ethics around marrying your sister off to a rapist just to convert some strangers to your religion?" said the boy. "That's a heavy balance to weigh."

"Especially at thirteen," said the man.

"Jeez, is *that* how old she is?"

"Approximately. Just wait until you see how it unfolds."

"Well quit dilly-dallying, old-timer."

The old man smiled. "Hamor and Shechem go back to their city and tell all the men that their neighbors have agreed to intermarry and live in peace with them and trade, under one condition. But that condition is soon accepted as Hamor persuades them of the benefit in absorbing their population and property and animals into their own."

"I noticed the reason this all came to be was left out of the sales pitch," said the boy. "Really, though, what are the death rates of something like this? I noticed those were left out of Abraham's sales pitch for circumcision as well."

"What do you mean?" said the man.

"I mean in times without hygiene and sanitation a *city* full of men inflict a serious wound on themselves, and you think no one died of infection? I'm just noticing the text never said, 'And twenty percent of the men who agreed to God's covenant perished due to a mysterious discoloration spreading from their groin.' You know what I'm saying? Blame it on Satan or do what you gotta do, but let's not sweep the inevitable consequences of mass wound infliction under the rug."

"Keep in mind that a 'city' in these times could have meant a few hundred people," said the man. And with a growing smile he added, "But I think you're being impatient when it comes to the rate of death."

"Alright," said the boy, "let's hear it then."

So the man read:

Three days later, while all of them were still in pain, two of Jacob's sons, Simeon and Levi, Dinah's brothers, took their swords and attacked the unsuspecting city, killing every male.[159]

"Wow," said the boy. "Wow. Definitely didn't see that coming."

"Turns out Jacob's sons inherited their father's knack for deception," said the man, reading on again:

> They killed Hamor and his son Shechem with their swords, took Dinah from Shechem's house, and went away. Jacob's sons came to the slaughter and plundered the city because their sister had been defiled. They took their flocks, herds, donkeys, and whatever was in the city and in the field. They captured all their possessions, dependents, and wives and plundered everything in the houses.[160]

"I'm all for revenge," said the boy, "but using God's covenant as a bait and switch for genocide? I mean there's gotta be a special place in Hell for that sort of thing, right?"

"You probably won't like what Jacob has to say to his boys," said the man, reading on:

> "You have troubled me by making me obnoxious among the inhabitants of the land, among the Canaanites and the Perizzites, and since I am few in number, they will gather themselves together against me and kill me. I shall be destroyed, my household and I."
> But they said, "Should he treat our sister like a harlot?"[161]

"You've troubled me? Obnoxious? Never mind the fact that my daughter was just raped. I'm starting to dislike this guy as much as Abraham."

"This reaction certainly doesn't show Jacob in the best light," said the man. "I've looked for insight into this verse and found a few answers, though none of them leave you feeling satisfied. One is that while his initial reaction shows little concern for Dinah's violation, his greater concern is for the safety of all of his people, as well as God's prophecy, now that his sons have invoked the wrath of the surrounding tribes. While what happened to Dinah is upsetting, she may be raped a hundred times over and killed along with all his other children if Hamor's brethren seek revenge."

"I suppose that's true," said the boy, "although he does emphasize 'kill *me*' and '*I* shall be destroyed.'"

"I'm not defending his words," said the man, "just sharing what I've found. I don't believe Jacob is someone the average person might pick out as the hero of a story. Most of the Biblical heroes are riddled with humanity. These weren't even necessarily *good* people in any kind of divine sense."

"Yeah, they're more like rats dropped in a morality maze."

"Not exactly the words I would have chosen," said the man, "but you're certainly on to something there. God's chosen people are presented with ethical decisions that determine the course of our future."

"Either way," said the boy, "I think Leah's kids are beginning to realize where they stand in the order of most loved. They basically asked him, 'What the hell were *you* gonna do about it?'"

"Yes, it certainly appears Jacob is mostly passive as usual," said the man, "as we haven't heard anything from him since he learned of the news. Perhaps he left it to his sons to deal with intentionally but hadn't imagined they'd take it so far. Though, as we'll see, he doesn't do much to punish them for it either."

"He probably recognizes manipulation is in their blood at this point," said the boy. "The whole family's screwed up that way."

"Yes, well, this story also begs the question of where Leah was while her thirteen-year-old daughter was wandering around the neighboring tribes. And I've even heard some of the responsibility placed on Dinah's shoulders, venturing into a neighborhood she knows to be wicked."

"Oof. I don't know how I feel about that," said the boy. "All she did was go out and try to make some friends."

"I'm not saying I agree with it either," said the man, "and what happened to Dinah is inarguably awful, but what we have here is a cautionary tale about the realities of wandering into foreign streets on your own."

"The whole thing is a mess," said the boy. "Anyway, how do they deal with it?"

"Well, then God says to Jacob, 'Arise, go up to Bethel and dwell there, and make an altar there to God, who appeared to you when you fled from the face of Esau your brother.' Which is a good reminder of how the hero's journey is coming full circle," said the man, "as this is where he first landed when he ran away from home. And so he takes his people and journeys to

Bethel and builds an altar, where God appears to speak to Jacob again." The man looked down and read:

> "Your name is Jacob. No longer shall your name be called Jacob, but Israel shall be your name." So he called his name Israel.
>
> And God said to him, "I am God Almighty. Be fruitful and multiply. A nation and a company of nations shall come from you, and kings shall come from your own body. The land that I gave to Abraham and Isaac I will give to you, and I will give the land to your offspring after you."[162]

"So that's it, huh? Simeon and Levi take out a city full of innocent people and all God has to say is 'be fruitful and multiply'? Presumably with all the heathen widows they took captive? What happened to all that talk about men who shed blood will pay with bloodshed? God's chosen ones have turned into deceitful mass murderers and He just looks the other way?"

"This is true," said the man. "Genesis doesn't detail any punishment, nor approval of Levi and Simeon's actions here. There is no sense that God commanded this retaliation, and even if He had required the destruction of this city, we can guess it may have come in a similar manner to Sodom and Gomorrah. We'll see these two brothers suffer consequences later on, but for now, God refrains from inflicting any upon them. So what we're left with is another moral dilemma to chew on while balancing the desire for justice with the temptation to go overboard in revenge."

"I think 'overboard' is an understatement," said the boy.

"Their motivations were pure, but their actions surely broke the Lord's covenant. We'll get back to these brothers later though," said the man. "For now, God leaves Jacob, and Jacob makes a pillar of stone. He pours oil upon it and names it Bethel."

"I take it there's meaning to that name?" said the boy.

"House of God," said the man. "Then, on their journey onward, Rachel goes into labor, and she has a hard labor, one that ends in her demise. And as her soul was departing she names her son Ben-Oni, but Jacob names him Benjamin."

"Your beloved wife's dying breath is to name her last child one thing, and rather than say any parting words, you're like, 'Nah. I don't care for that one.' Please explain."

"First, let us note how Rachel once passionately declared, 'Give me children, or else I die!' And once she had children, she died."

"Oh wow," said the boy. "I would have forgotten that."

"But to your point," said the man, "the name Rachel chose means 'the son of my sorrow,' as the life of her son cost her her own. Jacob, I assume, not wishing to be reminded of his wife's painful death every time he calls on his son's name, changed it to mean 'the son of my right hand,' or someone very dear to me, perhaps to avoid any ill omen that may come along with the former choice. And as to his parting words to Rachel, we know the Bible spares many details, but I think we can assume from previous descriptions that this was a heartbreaking experience."

The boy lifted his water bottle and poured one out on the ground.

The man smiled and shook his head as he kept reading:

And Jacob set a pillar on her grave, which is the pillar of Rachel's grave to this day. Then Israel journeyed and pitched his tent beyond the tower of Eder. And it happened, when Israel dwelt in that land, that Reuben went and lay with Bilhah his father's concubine.[163]

"What," said the boy, "is wrong with these people? This book has more drama than a soap opera."

"Indeed it does," said the man, "which is very much the point regarding how many lessons we can derive from these stories. But here the Scripture leaves a frustrating lack of insight into the situation. The explanation I find most convincing revolves around the relationships between the parties involved. Reuben is the eldest son of Leah, the unloved wife of Jacob, and Bilhah is the maidservant of Rachel, the beloved wife of Jacob. The motivation could have been an innocent love affair, sure, but I think, considering the timing and circumstance, it was more likely an act of revenge. Now, how accepting Bilhah was to Reuben's advances is left to the imagination. Was this lust or love? Did she have a gripe against Rachel, or was Reuben merely forceful in this situation? My guess is forceful, as I'd like to imagine Bilhah was mourning her mistress, but I suppose we'll never know for sure."

"And how does Jacob react to all of this?"

"He doesn't," said the man.

The boy threw his hands in the air and said, "Typical!"

"All we know is that he 'heard about it' before the story carries on."

"Unbelievable, man."

"No more is said, and no more needs to be. I'm sure we can all fill in the blank regarding how Jacob must have felt about this betrayal in a time of mourning. Some people see his non-reaction as weakness, others as self-control, but either way we'll see how this affects their father-son relationship down the road."

"Alright, alright," said the boy. "Keep going then."

"Then Jacob rejoins his father Isaac at Mam—"

"Are you kidding me?" said the boy. "This dude is still alive? He was on his deathbed like thirty years ago."

"It's possible this is out of chronological order," said the man, "placed here to wrap up the chapter. Actually it's unclear whether or not Jacob ever exchanged any words with his father after he left home. All we know is that Isaac breathed his last breath and died at one hundred and eighty years old, and that Esau and Jacob buried him. The point of mention here is really to bring the generations of Isaac to a close."

"Did Rebekah get the Eve treatment?"

"No mention of Rebekah," said the man, "so we're lead to assume she passed in the time Jacob was gone."

"Typical," said the boy.

GENESIS 37-41

JOSEPH

Shall you indeed reign over us?
Or shall you indeed have dominion over us?
—Joseph's brothers

"You remember Joseph, right?"

"Yeah, yeah. Favorite son of Rachel at the back of the line."

"That's the one," said the man. "He becomes the primary focus in this last portion of Genesis."

"Alright," said the boy, "let's hear it."

"We tune in when Joseph is seventeen, feeding the flock with his brothers. We learn that Joseph 'brought a bad report of them to his father.'"

"Great. A tattletale," said the boy. "I hate him already."

"You're not alone," said the man. "It's made clear that Joseph is the favorite child, and his father makes him a special tunic of many colors, so his brothers hate him when they see their father favors Joseph."

"I would too," said the boy. "Clearly no one is learning a lesson about playing favorites."

"No, they're not, and the consequences will come again soon. But first, Joseph has a dream in which he tells his brothers the following," said the man:

> "There we were, binding sheaves of grain in the field. Suddenly my sheaf stood up, and your sheaves gathered around it and bowed down to my sheaf."[164]

"A tattletale *and* a narcissist?" said the boy. "Even better."

"There's no context as to why he initially shared this dream with his brothers. Perhaps there was a genuine curiosity to see what they thought, or a need for help interpreting things, but it's not clear his intention was to ignite his brother's jealousy, although that was the result. His brothers tell him, 'Shall you indeed reign over us? Or shall you indeed have dominion over us?' And they hate him even more, for what in their eyes is bragging about this prediction of fate. Then he has another dream, and he tells his brothers again, 'And this time, the sun, the moon, and the eleven stars bowed down to me.'"

"What a little shit," said the boy. "He deserves whatever's coming to him."

"Careful what you say," said the man. "But this time he tells his father, too, making it clear these astral bodies represent his family bowing down before him. And even his father scolds him for suggesting the entire family will grovel on their knees. 'What is this dream that you have dreamed?' he says. 'Shall your mother and I and your brothers indeed come to bow down to the earth before you?'"

"Isn't he Rachel's kid?"

"I suppose 'mother' could have implied either the spirit of the departed Rachel or the still-living Leah," said the man.

"Ah, okay," said the boy. "Keep going then."

"From there we see his brothers go to feed their father's flock in Shechem. So Israel sends Joseph to see if all is well with his brothers and tells him to bring back word. So Joseph heads to Shechem and a man finds him wandering around the fields looking lost. He asks Joseph what he's looking for and Joseph says, 'I am seeking my brothers. Please tell me where they are feeding their flocks.' And the man tells him they've left, but before they did he heard them say, 'Let us go to Dothan.'"

"Uh-oh," said the boy. "The tattletale coming to spy on his brothers in another one of those *cities*."

"The motivation to visit Dothan isn't clear, but it doesn't end well for Joseph either way," said the man, reading on:

> They saw him in the distance, and before he had reached them, they plotted to kill him.[165]

"That seems a bit drastic," said the boy. "I think I take back what I said."

"I had a feeling you would," said the man. "Wait till you hear what happens next."

"Alright, shoot."

So the man continued:

> They said to one another, "Here comes this dreamer. Come now, let us kill him and throw him into one of the pits. Then we will say that a fierce animal has devoured him, and we will see what will become of his dreams."
>
> But when Reuben heard it, he rescued him out of their hands, saying, "Let us not take his life." And Reuben said to them, "Shed no blood. Throw him into this pit here in the wilderness, but do not lay a hand on him."[166]

The man looked up and said, "Reuben says this so he can come back later and return Joseph to their father."

"Who is Reuben again?"

"Jacob's oldest son with Leah," said the man, "which brings up an interesting point. All the favoritism shined on Joseph should rightfully belong to Reuben, so it's curious as to why he's sticking up for him here. Not only is he protecting someone who's taken his place as the rightful heir, but rescuing Joseph and returning him to their father would betray the rest of his brothers by exposing their actions."

"I'm listening," said the boy.

So the man read on:

> So it came about, when Joseph reached his brothers, that they stripped Joseph of his tunic, the multicolored tunic that was on him, and they took him and threw him into the pit. Now the pit was empty, without any water in it. Then they sat down to eat a meal.[167]

"Jeez, don't let your brother rotting in some pit spoil your appetite now," said the boy.

The man continued:

They looked up and saw a caravan of Ishmaelites coming from Gilead. Their camels were loaded with spices, balm and myrrh, and they were on their way to take them down to Egypt.

Judah said to his brothers, "What will we gain if we kill our brother and cover up his blood? Come, let's sell him to the Ishmaelites and not lay our hands on him. After all, he is our brother, our own flesh and blood." His brothers agreed.[168]

"They *sell* their brother? These people are animals!"

"Indeed they are," said the man. "And when the traders pass by they pull Joseph from the pit and sell him to the Ishmaelites for twenty shekels of silver, and they take Joseph to Egypt."

"Alright, I definitely take back what I said."

The old man gave a nod. "It seems Reuben chose not to stay and eat with his brothers, because when he returns to the pit to fetch Joseph in secret later, he was gone. Reuben becomes heartbroken, and understandably so."

"Wait a minute," said the boy. "Wasn't this the son that slept with Jacob's concubine?"

"Yes, well—"

"*Pffft*. This guy was just trying to save face with his dad by rescuing the favorite son."

"Well it's possible he just loved his broth—"

"In this family? I don't think so, pal." The boy shook his head. "Keep going."

The old man smiled as he said, "So the brothers take Joseph's tunic, kill one of their goats, and dip it in blood. Then they bring it to their father." Then he looked down and read:

> "We have found this. Do you know whether it is your son's tunic or not?"
>
> And he recognized it and said, "It is my son's tunic. A wild beast has devoured him. Without doubt Joseph is torn to pieces."[169]

"And as you can expect," said the man, "Jacob didn't take the news too well. He mourns his son for many days, and when his children try to comfort him, he tells them he will mourn his son until the day he joins him in the grave."

"Ouch," said the boy.

"Ouch is right," said the man. "Meanwhile the traders sold Joseph in Egypt to Potiphar, an officer of Pharaoh and captain of the guard."

The boy noticed the man turn the page prematurely and begin reading from the bottom of the next:

> Now Joseph had been taken down to Egypt. And Potiph—

"Woah, woah, woah," said the boy. "What's happening here?"

"Well, Joseph was sold into slavery, remember?"

"No, no, no. I think you know what I mean."

"Oh, well, nothing important really," said the man.

But before he could finish speaking, the boy slid his hand under the book and turned it toward himself. He flipped to the prior page and began skim reading aloud. "Judah leaves his brothers and marries a Canaanite girl... They pop out a few kids... The first son marries, but God thinks he's wicked so He *kills* him for no apparent reason..?" said the boy, shaking his head. "Judah tells his next son to marry her and raise an heir for his brother..." said the boy with a face of confusion. "And what's going on here?" the boy asked. "It says when he went into her, he 'emitted' on the ground. What does that mean?"

The man blushed a bit and stumbled over his words. "Well, he, um, spills his, uh... Well he wastes his, uh..." The man paused and said, "Do you know what the term coitus interruptus means?"

"Oh, he pulled out," said the boy, skim reading on. "And this displeased the Lord, so the Lord *killed* him too..?" The boy looked up in surprise. "What? God killed someone because he didn't like being forced to knock up his wicked brother's wife?"

The old man drew in a deep breath as the boy stared blankly in his direction. He let out a long sigh before he began to explain. "Marrying a widow to the next brother in line was a custom passed down through tradition. The children born to this practice were seen as perpetuating the family line of the departed brother. When Onan wastes his, well, seed, he did so intentionally to deny his brother a family so that he would inherit Judah's property and livestock instead. He robbed his brother of his legacy, inheritance, and support for his wife. The Lord saw this act of greed as dishonorable."

"Dishonorable?" said the boy. "He brought His big thumb down and squashed him like an ant!"

"How Onan's life is cut short isn't detailed," said the man. "But, yes, the Lord of the Old Testament is often seen as harsher than the Lord of the New Testament."

"Levi and Simeon slit the throats of an entire town," said the boy. "Pulling out of a wicked man's wife you were forced to marry is worse than *that*?"

"Well, I've heard speculation that Onan used Tamar for sex, but rather than honoring her as his new wife and giving her the blessing of being a future mother, he 'pulled out,' as you say, treating her like some kind of prostitute. Can you find any morality in that?"

The boy had nothing to say.

"One of the reasons what's known as a 'levirate marriage' will later become part of Mosaic law is because a childless widow didn't have much of a place in ancient society. This practice was to protect a woman who'd already given up her virginity to a deceased husband." There was another awkward pause. "Again, I didn't write it," said the man. "I'm just sharing what I know about the context of the times."

"Here," said the boy, turning the Bible back to face the man, "you finish it. It can't get much worse."

The old man groaned. "It always seems to get worse."

"When do we get to the *holy* part of the Bible?" said the boy. "The beginning is pure chaos."

"It sure is," said the man, looking down to read again:

> Then Judah said to Tamar his daughter-in-law, "Remain a widow in your father's house, till Shelah my son grows up," for he feared that he would die like his brothers. So Tamar went and remained in her father's house.[170]

"Judah's probably starting to think *all* his descendants will be cursed."

The man paused for a moment as he thought about it. "We'll get there," he said. "Anyway, as time goes on, Judah's wife dies. After he recovers from the grief he goes up to Timnah to shear his sheep. When Tamar hears of this, she changes out of her widow's clothes and covers her face with a veil. By this time she's realized Judah's youngest son had grown up and hadn't been given to her as a husband, out of his father's fear he'd die like his brothers. So she goes to sit at the open road on the way to Timnah." The man looked down to read once more:

> When Judah saw her, he thought she was a harlot, because she had covered her face.
>
> Then he turned to her by the way, and said, "Please let me come in to you," for he did not know that she was his daughter-in-law.
>
> So she said, "What will you give me, that you may come in to me?"
>
> And he said, "I will send a young goat from the flock."
>
> So she said, "Will you give me a pledge till you send it?"

Then he said, "What pledge shall I give you?"

So she said, "Your signet and cord, and your staff that is in your hand."

Then he gave them to her, and went in to her.[171]

"I smell trouble," said the boy.

"Yes, well, Tamar becomes pregnant from that exchange," said the man, "which I'll get to momentarily. But first Tamar returns home and changes back into her widow's clothes, so when Judah sends his friend to exchange the promised goat and take back his pledge, he can no longer find her. He asks the locals where he can find the harlot of Timnah and they tell him there is no such harlot around. He stops the search and chalks his staff and signet up to a loss to spare his reputation the mark of sleeping with a harlot, not to mention so soon after the death of his wife."

The boy shook his head. "Well that's what he gets for trusting some *strumpet* with his most valuable object."

The man tried to hold back a smile. "Yes, but three months later Judah's informed that Tamar has become pregnant by means of prostitution, so Judah says, 'Bring her out and let her be burned!'"

"Jeez!" said the boy. "That seems harsh."

"Not to mention hypocritical," said the man. "But clever Tamar shows Judah the seal and staff and says, 'By the man to whom these belong, I am with child.' So Judah acknowledges what's happened and he says, 'She has been more righteous than I, because I did not give her to Shelah my son.'"

"Got 'em," said the boy. "What a mess though. Everyone loves to come up with these crazy schemes."

"They do indeed," said the man, reading on again:

When the time came for her to give birth, there were twin boys in her womb. As she was giving birth, one of them put out his hand, so the midwife took a scarlet thread and tied it on his wrist and said, "This one came out first." But when he drew back his hand, his brother came out, and she said, "So this is how you have broken out!"[172]

"And his name was called Perez," said the man, "meaning breach or burst forth. And after, his brother was born with the scarlet thread on his hand, and his name was called Zerah."

"What does that one mean?"

"I've found things like 'dawn' or 'rising' or 'brightness,'" said the man, "but none of them exactly seem fitting."

"They sound like they're words describing the sun," said the boy. "Maybe it's a play on how the sun will show itself temporarily and then disappear again."

The man's eyebrows perked up. "You know, that's not half bad."

"Call me a scholar," said the boy.

The man smiled and said, "Now from here we go to Egypt. If you recall, Joseph was purchased by Pharaoh's captain of the guard, Potiphar." The man looked down and read:

The Lord was with Joseph so that he prospered, and he lived in the house of his Egyptian master. When his master saw that the Lord was with him and that the Lord gave him success in everything he did, Joseph found favor in his eyes and became his attendant. Potiphar put him in charge of his household, and he entrusted to his care everything he owned. From the time he put him in charge of his household and of all that he owned, the Lord blessed the household of the Egyptian because of Joseph. The blessing of the Lord was on everything Potiphar had, both in the house and in the field. So Potiphar left everything he had in Joseph's care. With Joseph in charge, he did not concern himself with anything except the food he ate.[173]

"What does that last line mean?"

"It means Potiphar didn't have to concern himself with anything but food because he trusted Joseph so much to run his affairs."

"Ah, okay," said the boy.

So the man read on:

Now Joseph was handsome in form and appearance. And after a time his master's wife cast her eyes on Joseph and said, "Lie with me."[174]

"Oh brother," said the boy. "The drama never stops."

"No," said the man, "seems it doesn't. But it's difficult to overstate the position this puts Joseph in. Normally a slave would have to obey his master's wife, but here, of course, this command would cause Joseph to commit a betrayal of his master."

"Here comes the tattletale," said the boy.

"Not exactly," said the man. "Joseph refuses her advances day after day, asking how he could commit such wicked sin against his Lord. But on one occasion, Joseph was working when no one else was around and she grabs his garment saying, 'Lie with me.' But he leaves his garment behind and runs away. Clearly upset by the ongoing rejection, Potiphar's wife calls the men of the house and tells them he tried to force himself upon her, saying when she yelled for help he left his garment and ran. When her husband returns, she tells him the same story and he was furious, so he threw Joseph in jail."

The man looked up and saw anger brewing in the boy's eyes. "What is it?"

"Nothing."

"Nothing?" said the man. "You seem pretty upset about something."

"It's nothing," said the boy. "This story just strikes a personal chord, that's all."

"Care to explain?" said the man.

"I don't know. It's a pretty sensitive topic these days."

The man looked over his shoulder to the left, then over his other shoulder to the right. Then he looked back at the boy. "I don't see any sensitive people around here."

The boy hesitated for a moment longer, but then he spoke. "I had this friend who graduated before me. His freshman year at college he hooked up with a girl in his dorm one night after they'd both been drinking. The next day the police showed up to interrogate him, saying the girl claimed she'd been raped. He was shocked. Everyone was shocked. They looked into the case and there were all these texts on the girl's phone saying she was coming over and wanted to hook up. There were even texts with her friends saying she was going to his place to get laid. The guy had no track record of anything like this before and plenty of people came to his defense saying he wasn't that kind of guy. I mean I knew the guy and he'd never do anything like that. But despite all the evidence, they arrested him and kicked him out of school. They ruined his whole life because of this girl's claim!"

The man remained silent to allow the boy to finish, but when it appeared he had nothing more to say, he spoke. "As they say, there are three sides to every story, perspective A, perspective B, and the truth. But it doesn't seem fair there wasn't any kind of due process in this situation."

"None," said the boy. "They just took her side because she's a girl and conjured tears. And look, there's no way I can say for sure he didn't do anything. Maybe things started and she wanted to stop and he kept going, or something like that, but what happened to innocent until proven guilty? They fuck up a guy's life when all the evidence points to the contrary?"

"What motivation do you think she'd have for lying?" said the man.

"What motivation does any woman have to lie about anything?" said the boy. "Maybe somebody found out and started teasing her. Maybe she thought it was a good idea when she was drunk but sobered up and regretted it. Maybe he had a tiny dick and came in two seconds and she never wanted to see him again. Or maybe he flat out rejected her like Joseph did and she wanted to make him pay. Are you trying to convince me no woman has ever justified lying about anything? That we have to believe all women just because they have a vagina? That amongst the *billions* of them that have existed throughout history not a single one has bent the truth to screw over a man?"

"That's not exactly what I was getting at," said the man. "But wome—"

"This isn't even about women! It's about liars, and truth. And in this case there was no evidence to prove what was truth and what was a lie. But that doesn't mean you just pick sides because of a gender and ruin someone's life. Take it to court, bring them in front of a jury or whatever you have to do. And if more women come out and say he did that to them as well, then okay, we have a case. But if a bunch of guys come out and say she lied about them as well, maybe we can start to see a fucking pattern. But we don't play gender favorites with someone's future on the line without facts and stories."

"Well, there are surely plenty of cases like this where the truth is being told," said the man. "And in this case, we'll likely never know what happened, but I can see why you're upset."

"That's not the point," said the boy. "It just changes the whole legal system, ya know? It's not about whether you're a genuine human being or a liar, all that matters is what you have between your legs. It's the same thing in divorce courts."

"Well, I don—"

"I don't wanna talk about this anymore. It just caught me off guard to hear the Bible talk about it a thousand years ago and it's still relevant today. Let's just move on."

"You sure?" said the man. "I'm here if you need to vent."

"I'm sure," said the boy. "Keep reading before I really start ranting."

"Alright. But just know this won't be the last thing that occurred long ago that still applies today." The boy nodded, so the man drew in a long breath before looking down to read again:

> The Lord was with him, he showed him kindness and granted him favor in the eyes of the prison warden. So the warden put Joseph in charge of all those held in the prison, and he was made responsible for all that was done there. The warden paid no attention to anything under Joseph's care, because the Lord was with Joseph and gave him success in whatever he did.[175]

The man looked up to see the boy still visibly upset. "If you're listening, this is a good place to see that Joseph could have responded by withdrawing into himself, or cursing the Lord who allowed him to be sold into slavery and jailed, but instead he chose to serve others with integrity as a man who believed he was blessed. And in return, God gave him favor in the sight of the warden, a good reminder that God can raise up friends in places even where we don't expect them. This is the second time Joseph could have been killed, but instead he was given an opportunity to work through his adversity and rise up again."

The boy didn't say anything, but his anger began to melt away, so the man kept reading:

> Some time later, the cupbearer and the baker of the king of Egypt offended their master, the king of Egypt. Pharaoh was angry with his two officials, the chief cupbearer and the chief baker, and put them in custody in the house of the captain of the guard, in the same prison where Joseph was confined. The captain of the guard assigned them to Joseph, and he attended them.[176]

"Wait," said the boy, "didn't you say Potiphar was captain of the guard?"

"Well, when the Bible says 'some time later' we're unsure of exactly how much time has gone by. If it's years, perhaps Potiphar has moved on from his position. But if it's still him, perhaps he begins to see Joseph in a good light again. If so, for the sake of his own peace and his wife's reputation, Joseph remains in jail."

The boy nodded, so the man read on:

> While they were in prison, Pharaoh's cupbearer and baker each had a dream one night, and each dream had its own meaning. When Joseph saw them the next morning, he noticed that they both looked upset.[177]
>
> So he asked Pharaoh's officials who were in custody with him in his master's house, "Why do you look so sad today?"[178]
>
> They said to him, "We have had dreams, and there is no one to interpret them."
>
> And Joseph said to them, "Do not interpretations belong to God? Please tell them to me."[179]

"That's a bit presumptuous," said the boy, "considering where his last interpretation got him."

The man smiled and kept reading:

So the chief cupbearer told his dream to Joseph and said to him, "In my dream there was a vine before me, and on the vine there were three branches. As soon as it budded, its blossoms shot forth, and the clusters ripened into grapes. Pharaoh's cup was in my hand, and I took the grapes and pressed them into Pharaoh's cup and placed the cup in Pharaoh's hand."

Then Joseph said to him, "This is its interpretation: the three branches are three days. In three days Pharaoh will lift up your head and restore you to your office, and you shall place Pharaoh's cup in his hand as formerly, when you were his cupbearer. Only remember me, when it is well with you, and please do me the kindness to mention me to Pharaoh, and so get me out of this house. For I was indeed stolen out of the land of the Hebrews, and here also I have done nothing that they should put me in prison."[180]

"Notice he doesn't accuse either his brethren or his mistress for his circumstance," said the man, "but merely asserts his own innocence."

"Am I supposed to take that as some kind of nobility?"

"I think it says something about his character, yes. Anyway," said the man:

When the chief baker saw that the interpretation was favorable, he said to Joseph, "I also had a dream. There were three cake baskets on my head, and in the uppermost basket there were all sorts of baked food for Pharaoh, but the birds were eating it out of the basket on my head."

And Joseph answered and said, "This is its interpretation. The three baskets are three days. In three days Pharaoh will lift up your head from you and hang you on a tree. And the birds will eat the flesh from you."[181]

Pharaoh's birthday came three days later, and he prepared a banquet for all his officials and staff. He summoned his chief cup-bearer and chief baker to join the other officials. He then restored the chief cup-bearer to his former position, so he could again hand Pharaoh his cup. But Pharaoh impaled the chief baker, just as Joseph had predicted when he interpreted his dream. Pharaoh's chief cup-bearer, however, forgot all about Joseph, never giving him another thought.[182]

The boy was taking a sip of water and began coughing wildly, pounding a fist on his chest.

"You alright?" said the man.

"What the hell?" the boy croaked between coughs. "How could you forget about something like that?"

"My guess is the failure to mention this was likely on purpose," said the man. "Perhaps he thought the timing to stir up more controversy for Pharaoh wasn't right immediately upon his release."

"Well," said the boy, still clearing his throat, "I guess we'll be seeing Joseph's brothers bowing down soon."

The man smiled again and read on:

Two full years later, Pharaoh dreamed that he was standing on the bank of the Nile River. In his dream he saw seven fat, healthy cows come up out of the river and begin grazing in the marsh grass. Then he saw seven more cows come up behind them from the Nile, but these were scrawny and thin. These cows stood beside the fat cows on the riverbank. Then the scrawny, thin cows ate the seven healthy, fat cows! At this point in the dream, Pharaoh woke up.

But he fell asleep again and had a second dream. This time he saw seven heads of grain, plump and beautiful, growing on a single stalk. Then seven more heads of grain appeared, but these were shriveled and withered by the east wind. And these thin heads swallowed up the seven plump, well-formed heads! Then Pharaoh woke up again and realized it was a dream.

The next morning Pharaoh was very disturbed by the dreams. So he called for all the magicians and wise men of Egypt. When Pharaoh told them his dreams, not one of them could tell him what they meant.[183]

The boy coughed one last time. "Sorry."

"No worries," said the man. "Anyway, here's where the butler speaks up regarding Joseph. He tells Pharaoh about his time spent in prison and the interpretations of his dream, so Pharaoh sends for Joseph, and when he stands before him, Pharaoh tells him about the dream."

"Two years later," said the boy. "Thanks, butler."

"Well, he could have rot in there forever," said the man, "or been hanged. But we also need to have patience until the timing is right for God's plan to unfold. Had the butler told Pharaoh of

Joseph upon his release, perhaps he would have been let go and sent home to the land of Hebrews. But wait another two years and misfortune turns to fortune that he wouldn't have otherwise been granted, as we'll see now."

"Alright, let's see it then," said the boy.

"Right then. Here's Joseph's interpretation," said the man:

"The dreams of Pharaoh are one and the same. God has revealed to Pharaoh what He is about to do. The seven good cows are seven years, and the seven good heads of grain are seven years. It is one and the same dream. The seven lean, ugly cows that came up afterward are seven years, and so are the seven worthless heads of grain scorched by the east wind. They are seven years of famine. It is just as I said to Pharaoh. God has shown Pharaoh what He is about to do.

"Seven years of great abundance are coming throughout the land of Egypt, but seven years of famine will follow them. Then all the abundance in Egypt will be forgotten, and the famine will ravage the land. The abundance in the land will not be remembered, because the famine that follows it will be so severe. The reason the dream was given to Pharaoh in two forms is that the matter has been firmly decided by God, and God will do it soon.

"And now let Pharaoh look for a discerning and wise man and put him in charge of the land of Egypt. Let Pharaoh appoint commissioners over the land to take a fifth of the harvest of Egypt during the seven years of abundance. They should collect all the food of these good years that are coming and store up the grain under the authority of Pharaoh, to be kept in the cities for food. This food should be held in reserve for the country, to be used during the seven years of famine that will come upon Egypt, so that the country may not be ruined by the famine."[184]

"Good timing on the whole 'select a wise man' play," said the boy, "right after all the other wise men failed."

"Precisely. And the advice is good in the eyes of Pharaoh, as we see in what he tells Joseph here," said the man, looking down at his Bible:

> "Since God has shown you all this, there is none so discerning and wise as you are. You shall be over my house, and all my people shall order themselves as you command. Only as regards the throne will I be greater than you."[185]

"Moving on up in the world I see," said the boy.

"Yes, well, we may not always see God's plan for us when things aren't going well, but in this case we see a swift turn in fortune as His plan unfolds."

"Promoted to rule over a kingdom as a slave," said the boy. "Must be nice to see the future."

"This seems to follow the pattern of Joseph's life where others entrust him with nearly all their responsibilities. And we'll see this position taken very seriously, as Pharaoh dresses Joseph in fine clothing and jewelry and parades him around in a chariot, telling his people to bow before him, giving Joseph power and control. Then Pharaoh names him Zaphnath-Paaneah, which means something like 'a revealer of secrets,' and then he gives him Asenath as a wife, the daughter of Poti-Pherah, priest of On."

"And how old was he at this point?"

"Thirty at the time the prophecy begins to unfold," said the man. "And in the seven years before the famine, he stored immeasurable amounts of grain in every city. And in these years his wife gave birth to two sons, Manasseh, 'For God has made me forget all my toil and all my father's house,' and Ephraim, 'For God has caused me to be fruitful in the land of my affliction.' Then the seven years of abundance end and the seven years of famine begin. And the famine exists throughout all the surrounding lands, but in Egypt there was bread because of Joseph, and Joseph was able to open the storehouses and sell his bread to the Egyptians, as well as the rest of the surrounding world who came to Egypt for grain."

"I suppose this is the origin of that moral about saving a penny for a rainy day?" said the boy.

"Well, a drought, in this case," said the man, "but perhaps so."

GENESIS 42-45

BROTHERS IN EGYPT

And as for you,
go up in peace to your father.
—Joseph

"When Jacob hears there is grain in Egypt he says to his sons, 'Why do you look at one another?'"

"Yeah," said the boy, "*do* something!"

"Precisely," said the man. "In Jacob's growing age he becomes unusually impatient, and he tells his sons to 'go down to that place and buy for us there, that we may live and not die.'"

"Seems like a pretty good idea," said the boy.

"So Joseph's brothers go down to buy grain in Egypt, but Jacob doesn't send Joseph's younger brother Benjamin in fear something may happen to him."

"He probably thinks his second favorite son would disappear like Rachel's first," said the boy.

"That's right," said the man. "So Jacob's sons go to Egypt, and when they find the man who sold grain to the people they bowed their heads before him. Joseph recognizes them immediately, of course, but he pretends to be a stranger because they don't recognize him. He speaks to them harshly and says, 'Where do you come from?' To which they reply saying they traveled from the land of Canaan to buy food. Then Joseph remembers his dreams, but instead of revealing himself he says, 'You are spies! You have come to see the nakedness of the land!' Meaning its defenseless positions in these times."

"Burn them!" said the boy. "*Burn* them!"

"Actually you're not so far off," said the man. "In those times, spies would have been put to death for the sake of national security. It would have been easy for Joseph to take revenge on all his brothers at once, but revenge isn't what he's after."

"Well, what is he after?"

"You'll see," said the man. "So Joseph's brothers plead with this governor of Egypt, saying they are not spies but honest men, and all one man's sons who have come to buy food. But Joseph carries on with his ruse, saying, 'No, but you have come to see the nakedness of the land.'"

"Seems like a reasonable accusation," said the boy, "considering the surrounding nations know Egypt is the only one with food."

"Reasonable indeed. But here's how his brothers respond," said the man:

"Your servants were twelve brothers, the sons of one man, who lives in the land of Canaan. The youngest is now with our father, and one is no more."

Joseph said to them, "It is just as I told you. You are spies! And this is how you will be tested. As surely as Pharaoh lives, you will not leave this place unless your youngest brother comes here. Send one of your number to get your brother. The rest of you will be kept in prison, so that your words may be tested to see if you are telling the truth. If you are not, then as surely as Pharaoh lives, you are spies!"[186]

"Then he throws them all in prison for three days."

"I mean he's probably skeptical they didn't sell Benjamin into slavery like they did him," said the boy. "Jacob doesn't trust them, Joseph doesn't trust them. This doesn't say much about the state of this family."

"Ah, very good," said the man. "We'll get to that shortly. But before we do, on the third day Joseph tells his brothers that they can leave, and to take their grain back home, but he says one of them must stay behind until their youngest brother is brought before him to prove they aren't lying. Only then shall they all live. And so the brothers talk amongst themselves regarding what happened with Joseph years before, saying, 'We are truly guilty concerning our brother, for we saw the anguish of his soul when he pleaded with us, and we would not hear, therefore this distress has come upon us.'"

"Seems like a few days in jail gave them some time to think about what karma's brought around," said the boy.

"Even the passing of twenty years cannot bury what a guilty conscience holds onto," said the man. "Though they concealed their deed from men, God sees all."

The boy agreed with a nod.

"Anyway, Reuben says to his brothers, 'Didn't I tell you not to sin against the boy? But you didn't listen. So now there comes a reckoning for his blood.'"

"What's that mean exactly?"

"It means a reckoning is required for their brother's blood on their hands."

"Seems like Reuben is just trying to comfort himself," said the boy. "Probably overcompensating for the extra guilt of sleeping with his father's concubine."

"Yes," said the man, "often the most insecure is the loudest in the room. But here we learn the conversation was being held amongst the brothers in their native tongue, that Joseph had been using an interpreter to speak with them prior. But obviously Joseph can understand when he hears these admissions of guilt. So he turns himself away from them and weeps, because he was hearing for the first time that at least one of his brothers tried to save him."

"Yeah, that or because he hears the other nine brothers wanted to *kill* him."

"That's your glass half empty, my boy."

"Well, good for him then. I'm not sure I would have been so forgiving."

"Keep in mind, twenty years have passed where Joseph has gone through many ups and downs. By this time he must have been missing his family deeply, regardless of what had been done. He was likely starting to wonder if he'd ever see them again," said the man. "We don't hear much about Joseph's feelings on the matter until they all come welling to the surface. It must have been immensely emotional, even healing, for Joseph to hear his brothers' remorse."

"Yeah, yeah, yeah," said the boy. "What's next?"

"Next, Joseph takes Simeon, the next oldest in line behind Reuben, and ties him up before their eyes. He does this either because of Reuben's innocence in the matter or because the eldest should be responsible for reporting to their father."

"Either way," said the boy, "he doesn't want them thinking Simeon will be too comfortable while they're gone."

"That's right," said the man. "Then Joseph takes his servant aside and gives the command to fill their sacks with grain, to restore every man's money to his sack, and to give them provisions for the journey. So the servant does so, and then the brothers pack up to leave for their journey home. But along the way, they break for camp and one of them opens their sack to feed his donkey and sees the money returned. He says to his brothers, 'My money has been restored, and there it is, in my sack!' And their hearts fail them as they become afraid, saying to one another, 'What is this that God has done to us?'"

"Burn them!" said the boy. "*Burn* them!"

"Stealing from the governor of Egypt would certainly warrant a severe punishment," said the man, "but whether or not this was a trap set by Joseph in order to secure more accusations, or merely an act of kindness because he could never accept his father's money to feed his family, is not explicitly shared. Either way it has the effect of driving fear into his brothers' hearts, furthering their belief that God is punishing them for their previous deed. Here we can see a guilty conscience can interpret good fortune in a bad way."

"I vote for setting up further accusations," said the boy.

"I had a feeling you would," said the man. "So when they return to Jacob in Canaan they tell him what happened, informing their father that they must return with Benjamin in order to rescue Simeon. And when the rest of their brothers open their sacks and find each of their bundles of money, they become even more afraid." Then the man read:

> Their father Jacob said to them, "You have deprived me of my children. Joseph is no more and Simeon is no more, and now you want to take Benjamin. Everything is against me!"[187]
>
> Then Reuben said to his father, "Kill my two sons if I do not bring him back to you. Put him in my hands, and I will bring him back to you."[188]

"Wow," said the boy. "Tell the guy obsessed with losing sons that if you don't return his other favorite child he can go ahead and snap the necks of his grandchildren. That'll calm him down. That'll make up for the fact that you slept with his concubine."

"Yes, well, no one ever said Reuben was the brightest of Jacob's children. And apparently Jacob didn't care for this desperate attempt to get back in his good graces either. He tells him, 'My son shall not go down with you, for his brother is dead, and he is left alone. If any calamity should befall him along the way in which you go, then you would bring down my gray hair with sorrow to the grave.'"

"I like how he refers to Benjamin as 'my son,'" said the boy, "like the rest of you chumps are chopped liver."

"Yes, the insensitivity of Jacob's favoritism is astonishing. 'He is left alone' doesn't say much about the rest of his children either. But this may be an indication of suspicion that these older brothers had something to do with the disappearance of Joseph. He doesn't exactly trust them with Rachel's only other child now, does he?"

"No," said the boy, "he doesn't. So what happens?"

The man read:

Now the famine was severe in the land. And when they had eaten the grain that they had brought from Egypt, their father said to them, "Go again, buy us a little food."[189]

"I love how they just sit around for months stuffing their faces before they remember, 'Oh yeah! Our other brother is still

GENESIS

tied up in a dungeon somewhere!' This family is a real piece of work."

"Keep in mind, a journey conveyed in a few words here is many days there. This wasn't like driving down to your county jail to put up Simeon's bail. Also, they had to feed numerous families with what little they carried on their backs on the first trip. We can assume the amount of time that passed was on the shorter end, not the longer."

"Mhm," said the boy. "Let's hear it then."

So the man continued:

But Judah said to him, "The man solemnly warned us, saying, 'You shall not see my face unless your brother is with you.' If you will send our brother with us, we will go down and buy you food. But if you will not send him, we will not go down, for the man said to us, 'You shall not see my face, unless your brother is with you.'"

Israel said, "Why did you treat me so badly as to tell the man that you had another brother?"

They replied, "The man questioned us carefully about ourselves and our kindred, saying, 'Is your father still alive? Do you have another brother?' What we told him was in answer to these questions. Could we in any way know that he would say, 'Bring your brother down'?"[190]

"That's not how it happened," said the boy. "They coughed up that information on their own."

"That detail may be true," said the man. "But they had no reason to lie to the Egyptian governor when being charged with those accusations. Perhaps they were trying to paint a little humanity around themselves as a plea for compassion to spare their lives. They were desperately trying to show their innocence as honest men."

"Yeah, well, they weren't exactly honest here," said the boy.

"I think we'll have to let it slide," said the man, reading on again:

> Judah said to his father, "Send the boy with me, and we will be on our way. Otherwise we will all die of starvation, and not only we, but you and our little ones. I personally guarantee his safety. You may hold me responsible if I don't bring him back to you. Then let me bear the blame forever. If we hadn't wasted all this time, we could have gone and returned twice by now."[191]

"Ah, so it's Jacob's fault they were dragging their feet this time."

"Yes, it appears Judah is the one to express some urgency in the situation now. Jacob's fear and favoritism seems to put the family at risk of starvation, only giving in when faced with running out of food. But Judah's words seem to convince his father, based on Jacob's response here," said the man:

> "If it must be so, then do this. Take some of the best fruits of the land in your vessels and carry down a present for the man, a little balm and a little honey, spices and myrrh, pistachio nuts and almonds. Take double money in your hand, and take back in your hand the money that was returned in the mouth of your sacks, perhaps it was an oversight. Take your brother also, and arise, go

back to the man. And may God Almighty give you mercy before
the man, that he may release your other brother and Benjamin. If
I am bereaved, I am bereaved!"[192]

"Looks like Benjamin might become the 'son of my sor-
rows' after all," said the boy.

"Yes, Jacob has a lot on the line here, so he makes sure to
send his sons off with gifts in addition to returning the money.
Perhaps in youth he would have kept it, but in old age he's
learned that when fortune comes to us by the mistake of others,
it deserves restitution. Though we receive it by oversight, keep-
ing it falls under dishonesty."

"At least someone has learned a lesson so far."

"Finally," said the man. "So Jacob's sons take the gifts and
Benjamin down to Egypt to see Joseph once more. When Joseph
sees them with Benjamin he tells the steward of his house, 'Take
these men to my home, and slaughter an animal and make ready,
for these men will dine with me at noon.' But when the time
comes to enter Joseph's house, the brothers were afraid, thinking
they were being led to an ambush, to be charged with the accusations of stealing the money and then enslaved. They explained
to the steward what happened and told him they've returned with
all the money as well as doubly more to buy food again, but the
steward surprises them by saying not to fear, that he'd received
their money the first time. Then he brings Simeon out to meet
them and gives them water to wash their feet and even feeds their
donkeys."

"Well that must've been a relief," said the boy.

"I imagine so. And with this they prepare their gifts for Joseph's arrival at noon. And when Joseph arrives, they bow before him and present their gifts. So Joseph asks about their and their father's well-being," said the man, reading the next line:

"Is your old father well, of whom you spoke? Is he still alive?"

And they said, "Your servant our father is well, he is still alive." Then they bowed down again in homage.

And as he raised his eyes and saw his brother Benjamin, his mother's son, he said, "Is this your youngest brother, of whom you spoke to me?" Then he said, "May God be gracious to you, my son."[193]

"So while Joseph's older brothers seek favor in Joseph, the lord of the land, Joseph directs Benjamin's favor toward God, the lord of lords. And then his heart yearns for his brother Benjamin, and he has to excuse himself again to weep."

"Big crybaby," said the boy. "Keep it together, man."

The old man said, "Keep in mind, he never knew if he'd see his mother's only other son again." Then he read on:

Then he washed his face and came out, and he restrained himself, and said, "Serve the bread." So they set him a place by himself, and them by themselves, and the Egyptians who ate with him by themselves, because the Egyptians could not eat food with the Hebrews, for that is an abomination to the Egyptians.[194]

"Does Joseph have to sit alone because he's a Hebrew?"

"At this point he's long absorbed into Egyptian culture," said the man, "so I think it's more likely because he's a minister of the state, unlikely to eat with Egyptians below him in class."

"Ah, okay. That makes sense," said the boy.

So the man read on:

Now they were seated before him, from the firstborn according to his birthright to the youngest according to his youth, and the men looked at one another in astonishment.[195]

"Why? What does that mean?"

"As if by some supernatural insight, the governor of Egypt, a stranger to their family, or so they think, has arranged their family in order of age."

"Ohhh, right," said the boy.

"He then goes a step further by serving Benjamin a portion five times the size of theirs, a custom meant to distinguish a special guest of honor."

"So Joseph's testing his brothers to see if the favored youngest inspires murderous jealousy again."

"Yes indeed," said the man. "But the text says they drank and were merry with him, so from what he could see, it did not. And after the feast, Joseph commands the steward to fill the men's sacks with as much food as they could carry, but then he also tells him to put each man's money in the mouth of his sack again. Then he instructs the steward to place his silver cup in the mouth of Benjamin's sack along with the money."

"Uh-oh," said the boy. "I smell a plan stewing."

"Your nose doesn't deceive you, for when morning dawns the brothers are sent away, and just when they are out of the city limits, Joseph sends his steward after them to hatch his plan. The steward rides up to stop and question them here," said the man:

> "Why have you repaid good with evil? Isn't this the cup my master drinks from and also uses for divination? This is a wicked thing you have done."

> But they said to him, "Why does my lord say such things? Far be it from your servants to do anything like that! We even brought back to you from the land of Canaan the silver we found inside the mouths of our sacks. So why would we steal silver or gold from your master's house? If any of your servants is found to have it, he will die, and the rest of us will become my lord's slaves."[196]

"Probably Reuben opening his big mouth again."

"Perhaps so," said the man. "So the steward agrees but lessens the terms. He says, 'Now also let it be according to your words, he with whom it is found shall be my slave, and you shall be blameless.' Then each man opens his sack and the steward searches them, beginning with the oldest, ending with the youngest."

"And of course it was in Benjamin's sack," said the boy.

"Of course," said the man. "So they were forced to return to the city. And when they arrive back at Joseph's house he says to them, 'What deed is this you have done? Did you not know that such a man as I can certainly practice divination?' Which, of course, he doesn't. He is merely playing this role of an Egyptian official to drive fear into their hearts."

"Seems like it's working," said the boy.

"It sure is. But then Judah speaks up and tells him this," said the man:

"Oh, my lord, what can we say to you? How can we explain this? How can we prove our innocence? God is punishing us for our sins. My lord, we have all returned to be your slaves. All of us, not just our brother who had your cup in his sack."[197]

But [Joseph] said, "Far be it from me that I should do so. The man in whose hand the cup was found, he shall be my slave. And as for you, go up in peace to your father."[198]

"Smart," said the boy. "Here's the real test of whether or not they're willing to sacrifice another brother to benefit themselves."

"Precisely," said the man. "Joseph isn't going to reveal himself to the same foolish brothers who will go on repeating their same evil deeds wherever they go. He needs to know if they've learned from their mistakes and grown, to see if there's hope in reuniting this family."

"And if not," said the boy, "Benjamin is probably better off with Joseph anyway."

"Likely so," said the man. "And notice the use of the line, 'And as for you, go up in peace to your father,' as he knows there will be no peace for them if Benjamin is not returned."

"Rubs their noses right in it," said the boy.

"Just think though," said the man, "they could go back to their father with a free conscience. And when Jacob asks where his favorite son is, they could have said, 'Your favorite son was a fool! He stole a silver cup from Pharaoh's court and they put him to death!' They could have rid themselves of both the favorite sons and restored proper order of the birthright in the family, where there were no favorites, where there were no beloved sons, where no two children were named as if they were the only ones. 'What would you have had us done?' they could have said. 'Your beloved son was a thief! He did this to himself! Look how wrong you were to favor him!'"

"I guess that's all true," said the boy.

"But Judah couldn't bear the thought of it," said the man, "so he comes forth and says, 'O my lord, please let your servant speak a word in my lord's hearing, and do not let your anger burn against your servant, for you are even like Pharaoh.' Then he relays the series of events from his family's point of view, highlighting his father's reaction if something were to happen to his youngest son, saying it would surely kill his father for them to return without his favorite son. He reveals his promise to bear the blame before their father for the rest of his life, and therefore he offers himself to remain as a slave in the place of his youngest brother. But he does so for a stunning reason," said the man. "He's willing to sacrifice himself for the love of his father knowing that Jacob loves Benjamin more than he loves Judah. Now think about *that* for a moment."

236

There was a pause before the boy said, "I'm not gonna admit there's a tear coming to my eye, but that is pretty touching."

"There bloody well should be," said the man. "With all of the favoritism Jacob has been showering upon Joseph and Benjamin, Judah is willing to swallow years of sibling rivalry and sacrifice his own freedom, all for the love of his father and the unwillingness to watch him mourn a brother who is loved more than he is."

"Yeah," said the boy, "that is a tear-jerker."

"Joseph apparently feels the same way," said the man, looking down at the Bible:

> Then Joseph could not restrain himself before all those who stood by him, and he cried out, "Make everyone go out from me!" So no one stood with him while Joseph made himself known to his brothers. And he wept aloud, and the Egyptians and the house of Pharaoh heard it.
>
> Then Joseph said to his brothers, "I am Joseph. Does my father still live?" But his brothers could not answer him, for they were dismayed in his presence. And Joseph said to his brothers, "Please come near to me." So they came near. Then he said, "I am Joseph your brother, whom you sold into Egypt. But now, do not therefore be grieved or angry with yourselves because you sold me here, for God sent me before you to preserve life."[199]

"You can't help but wonder if he would have done the same for Canaan had his brothers not sold him into slavery," said the boy. "Then all the surrounding countries would have been coming to Canaan to make it a well-known trading post instead of Egypt."

"Perhaps Canaan didn't have the infrastructure or the land or the manpower that Egypt had," said the man. "Remember, Joseph alone didn't grow and farm and harvest enough wheat to feed those nations. He merely foresaw what was coming and was placed in a position of power to orchestrate his plan. Had he not been in jail for the butler to see his power of prophecy, and had Pharaoh not appointed him to a position of power where people had to listen to him, perhaps he would have been ridiculed, like the first time he interpreted dreams."

"I stand corrected," said the boy.

"The moral here is not around growing of food," said the man, "but around forgiveness. Sure, sinners should grieve and be angry over their sins, but leave it up to God to humble them by making good from their evil. And leave it up to us to see the light in God's ways and accept the apologies of others when they're offered. If we held one another accountable for every little thing all the time, without hope for forgiveness, then relationships would be impossible, because there would be no room for error."

"I'm gonna look past the fact that we're talking about selling someone into slavery," said the boy, "because I think the overall point you're making is a good one."

"Joseph finds his brothers humbled for their sins, mindful of their remorse, and respectful of their youngest brother, even when they had the chance to let him take the fall to save themselves. He sees they've learned their lesson and changed their ways."

"I get it," said the boy. "So what happens?"

"So Joseph says, 'For these two years the famine has been in the land, and there are still five years in which there will be neither plowing nor harvesting. And God sent me before you to preserve a posterity for you in the earth, and to save your lives by a great deliverance. So now it was not you who sent me here, but God, and He has made me a father to Pharaoh, and lord of all his house, and a ruler throughout all the land of Egypt.' Then he tells his brothers to return to Jacob and bring him to Egypt, to dwell in the land of Goshen with his children, and his children's children, and all of his flocks and herds, because there he can provide for all of them in the remaining years of famine. Then he falls on Benjamin's neck and he weeps, and then all of his brothe—"

"Yeah, yeah, yeah," said the boy. "They have a big weepy powwow. Next?"

"Next the news spreads throughout the house of Pharaoh that Joseph's brothers have arrived, and this pleases Pharaoh and he tells Joseph that he will give his father and his households the best of the land of Egypt to dwell. He even tells Joseph to give them carts to carry their wives and little ones and provisions for the journey. So Joseph does so, and he also gives each brother a change of garments, but to Benjamin he gives three hundred pieces of silver and five changes of garments."

"You have to wonder what all of this spoiling is doing to Benjamin's ego," said the boy.

"These gifts will serve as evidence to Jacob that Joseph has become as rich and powerful as his brothers have claimed," said the man. "So Joseph loads twenty donkeys with Egyptian goods and food as a gift for his father. Then he sends his brothers along on their journey back home."

JACOB IN EGYPT

Not so, my father,
for this one is the firstborn.
—Joseph

"When Joseph's brothers arrive back in Canaan they tell their father, 'Joseph is still alive, and he is governor over all the land of Egypt,' and Jacob's heart stops because he doesn't believe them. But when they tell him everything Joseph had said and show him the carts to carry him there, the spirit of Jacob is revived."

"I can only imagine," said the boy, "after twenty years of mourning a dead child. I have to think his sons are feeling some guilt resurface in the face of his reaction as well."

"I'm sure, although they don't exactly admit the extent of the whole story."

"That probably would've stopped his heart beyond reviving," said the boy.

"Perhaps so," said the man. "But instead Israel says, 'It's enough. My son Joseph is still alive. I will go and see him before I die.'"

"How old is he at this point?"

"Around one hundred and thirty," said the man. "But although his age was great for a long and taxing journey, his desire to see Joseph was greater."

"Not to mention the last time he traveled he lost Rachel," said the boy. "That's probably weighing on his mind."

"Perhaps, but he begins the journey nonetheless. And when they come to Beersheba he offers a sacrifice to God, and God comes to Jacob in the night to tell him this," said the man:

"I am God, the God of your father. Do not fear to go down to Egypt, for I will make of you a great nation there. I will go down with you to Egypt, and I will also surely bring you up again, and Joseph will put his hand on your eyes."[200]

"I take it that means Joseph will be the one to cover his eyes after he dies?"

"That's right," said the old man, reading on again:

Then Jacob arose from Beersheba, and the sons of Israel carried their father Jacob, their little ones, and their wives, in the carts which Pharaoh had sent to carry him. So they took their livestock and their goods, which they had acquired in the land of Canaan, and went to Egypt, Jacob and all his descendants with him.[201]

"And after they settled in Goshen," said the man, "Joseph rides his chariot to see them. And when he sees his father he falls on his neck and weeps a good long while. Then Jacob says to

Joseph, 'Now let me die, since I have seen your face, because you are still alive.'"

"I love how Jacob's eyes are dry as a bone," said the boy.

"What do you mean?"

"Well, when Joseph hugged Benjamin it said they both wept on each other's necks, but when Joseph saw Jacob there was a one-way stream of tears. All Jacob said was 'kill me.'"

"I think you need to see someone about these interpretations of yours."

The boy laughed. "Probably."

"Even if you're right," said the man, "perhaps we're supposed to imagine a sobbing son on the shoulder of a father stiffened by disbelief, too overcome with feeling to know how to respond. That is, until he can summon the words of being so happy he could die."

"Fine," said the boy, "we'll go with that one."

The old man rolled his eyes. Then he said, "From there Joseph tells his brothers he'll inform Pharaoh that his family has arrived and they have brought with them their flocks and herds. He instructs them that when Pharaoh asks about their occupation, they shall say their occupation has been with livestock since youth so that they may dwell in the land of Goshen, for shepherds are an abomination to the Egyptians."

"I'm guessing there's significance there?"

"While it's not entirely clear, one explanation is that the Egyptians, who utilized agriculture in a single place, considered the semi-nomadic herdsmen from the north inferior. Joseph's mention of a distaste for shepherds is pushing his brethren to emphasize their role in raising cattle, a more respectable species in Egyptian culture in that time. Perhaps Joseph is also working to make sure Pharaoh feels justified in giving his family such a large swath of land, assuring him they'll be able to support themselves throughout the famine if they reside Goshen."

"Gotcha," said the boy.

"I believe Joseph also desires that his people live separately from the Egyptians so they may be less influenced by the vices of Egyptian people, or even insulted by their malice. He could easily employ them under himself as farmers in the corn trade, or perhaps members of the court or the army, but special treatment could have exposed them to the envy of the Egyptian people, or perhaps tempted the Israelites to forget their ways and the land of Canaan. He would not summon his people to Egypt just to be trampled upon, so he wishes to have them continue their tradition on separate land."

"That makes sense," said the boy. "So what happens next?"

"Pharaoh asks their occupation as Joseph said, and they do as Joseph told them. Then they say, 'We have come to dwell in the land, because your servants have no pasture for their flocks, for the famine is severe in the land of Canaan. Now therefore, please let your servants dwell in the land of Goshen.' And Pharaoh speaks to Joseph and grants this desire, wisely maintaining the understanding that his family is there under Joseph's care, not Pharaoh's. But Pharaoh goes a step further and says, 'And if you know any competent men among them, then make them chief herdsmen over my livestock,' which would make his brothers official members of the court, affording them benefits not usually offered to immigrants."

"Why do I get the feeling that might come into play down the road?"

"You'll have to wait and see," said the man. "But then Joseph brings in his father before Pharaoh, and Jacob blesses Pharaoh."

"Jacob blesses Pharaoh?" said the boy. "Shouldn't it be the other way around?"

"Not only was this an act of civility, but also a feeling of religious duty. While Pharaoh might be greater in earthly wealth, Jacob was greater in the interest of the Lord. You'll see as the conversation unfolds, the dynamic is not the same as Jacob's sons before him, bowing and calling themselves his servants. Here Pharaoh asks Jacob how old he is, seemingly out of respect for his age, and Jacob speaks freely, openly, even negatively, the last of which is a tone that becomes characteristic in his later years. Here, listen," said the man:

> "The days of the years of my pilgrimage are one hundred and thirty years. Few and evil have been the days of the years of my life, and they have not attained to the days of the years of the life of my fathers in the days of their pilgrimage."[202]

"Evil?" said the boy. "Considering how the story began I think he's done alright for himself with his wealth and four wives."

With a sly smirk the old man said, "Well if it isn't Mr. Glass Half Empty coming around to see the light of day. While that might be true, let's not forget the murderous tension with his brother that loomed over his shoulder, years of unjust servitude to his uncle, his beloved wife dying prematurely, and his favorite son's supposed death. But you're right, he chooses to view life through a pessimistic lens when he could also see his good fortune and legacy, and now his family's safety with food in the land of Goshen during a famine."

The boy gave a nod, so the man read on:

> But there was no food in the entire region, for the famine was very severe. The land of Egypt and the land of Canaan were exhausted by the famine. Joseph collected all the silver to be found in the land of Egypt and the land of Canaan in exchange for the grain they were purchasing, and he brought the silver to Pharaoh's palace.
>
> When the silver from the land of Egypt and the land of Canaan was gone, all the Egyptians came to Joseph and said, "Give us food. Why should we die here in front of you? The silver is gone!"
>
> But Joseph said, "Give me your livestock. Since the silver is gone, I will give you food in exchange for your livestock."[203]

"What are they putting in that bread?" said the boy.

"What do you mean?"

"I mean you're gonna trade a whole cow that could be dried into a long-term supply of jerky for a loaf of bread that will go stale in a day? Seems like you'd get more meals out of live-stock."

"Perhaps the trade was for more meals in grain than from that of slaughter," said the man. "Or perhaps the beasts had become more of a burden in the sense there was nothing left to feed them in the famished land."

"I'll let it slide," said the boy. "Keep going."

"I think the point being driven home is that a man will trade all that he has in order to preserve his life in desperate times. As we see, they traded all their livestock in exchange for bread that year. Then listen to what they come back and say the following," said the man:

"We cannot hide from our lord the fact that since our money is gone and our livestock belongs to you, there is nothing left for our lord except our bodies and our land. Why should we perish before your eyes, we and our land as well? Buy us and our land in exchange for food, and we with our land will be in bondage to Pharaoh. Give us seed so that we may live and not die, and that the land may not become desolate."[204]

"Hope that bread was worth it," said the boy.

"These remarks about the land becoming desolate show how dire the situation had become. Unless the people could go on sowing grain in the land, nature would reclaim the land as wilderness. Joseph didn't even have to suggest any bargains himself this time. The people came to him with the idea of offering their land and servitude."

The boy sat quietly, looking unsatisfied, so the man read on:

So Joseph bought all the land of Egypt for Pharaoh. All the Egyptians sold him their fields because the famine was so severe, and soon all the land belonged to Pharaoh. As for the people, he made them all slaves, from one end of Egypt to the other. The only land he did not buy was the land belonging to the priests. They received an allotment of food directly from Pharaoh, so they didn't need to sell their land.[205]

"Politics at its finest," said the boy. "The little man suffers while the higher-ups prosper."

"It's a timeless tradition," said the man, reading on again:

Then Joseph said to the people, "Indeed I have bought you and your land this day for Pharaoh. Look, here is seed for you, and you shall sow the land. And it shall come to pass in the harvest that you shall give one-fifth to Pharaoh. Four-fifths shall be your own, as seed for the field and for your food, for those of your households and as food for your little ones."

So they said, "You have saved our lives. Let us find favor in the sight of my lord, and we will be Pharaoh's servants."

And Joseph made it a law over the land of Egypt to this day, that Pharaoh should have one-fifth, except for the land of the priests only, which did not become Pharaoh's.[206]

"See," said the boy, "things like this are where you lose me."

"How so?" said the man.

In a cheery voice, the boy said, "You've saved our lives and now we're happily enslaved! Hoorayyy!" In a more serious tone he said, "Here's what really happened. Government established a twenty percent tax which eventually people questioned, so they came up with a story to justify it." The boy tightened up an imaginary tie and put on his best political impersonation. "Well, you see, my simple-minded commoners. Way back in the day there was a big famine, and you peasants neglected to prepare. But we, the wise old government, were smart enough to stash bread away for an entire population for five years without even using preservatives. And when you went hungry, you looked to us to save you like the heroes we are, because not a single one of you was smart enough to figure out that a cow provides more meals than a loaf of bread. And when you had nothing left to trade, you agreed to give up your freedom in exchange for food conveniently just before the famine ended. This was all your idea and you have no one to blame but yourselves. Now pay up!"

The man stared blankly for a moment. "Your imagination never ceases to amaze me."

The boy playfully pounded a fist on the table and said, "This book has *Uncle Sam Publications* written all over it."

"The reduction of a population to serfdom wasn't meant to be seen as an act of cruelty," said the man, "but rather a display of Joseph's administrative prowess in the eyes of Pharaoh."

"Don't they say history's always written by the winners?"

"I think we agreed to put historical disputes aside for the sake of the story," said the man. The boy pulled a zipper across his lips and laced his fingers in front of him. "Besides, I think you're losing sight of how this is a tale of the *Israelites*, not the perspective of the Egyptian government and its people."

The boy said nothing, so the man read on:

> Now Israel lived in the land of Egypt, in Goshen, and they acquired property in it and were fruitful and became very numerous. And Jacob lived in the land of Egypt for seventeen years, so the length of Jacob's life was one hundred and forty-seven years.[207]

"What a guy," said the boy. "One day he's on his deathbed, seventeen years later he's thriving through a famine."

"Yes, it seems Jacob was so satisfied with Joseph's reunion that he found the strength to carry on. But it's worth noting that our time isn't up to us," said the man, "it's in God's hands. We die when God plans for it, not once we've reached a peak of pleasure or a valley of grief. This is also a good time to point out the symmetry of seventeen years in which Jacob cared for Joseph before he was sold into slavery, and now seventeen years in which Joseph cared for Jacob in the declining years of his life."

The boy whispered, "Magical."

The man shook his head with rolling eyes and read on:

> And when the time drew near that Israel must die, he called his son Joseph and said to him, "If now I have found favor in your sight, put your hand under my thigh and promise to deal kindly and truly with me. Do not bury me in Egypt, but let me lie with

my fathers. Carry me out of Egypt and bury me in their burying place."

And he said, "I will do as you have said."

Then he said, "Swear to me."

And he swore to him.[208]

"Yes, son, reach down and grab ahold of my ancient—"

"*Then* Jacob became sick. When Joseph hears of this news he takes his two sons to visit him. Jacob gathers the strength to sit up in bed and speak to Joseph here," said the man:

"God Almighty appeared to me at Luz in the land of Canaan and blessed me, and He said to me, 'Behold, I will make you fruitful and numerous, and I will make you a multitude of peoples, and will give this land to your descendants after you as an everlasting possession.' Now your two sons, who were born to you in the land of Egypt before I came to you in Egypt, are mine. Ephraim and Manasseh shall be mine, as Reuben and Simeon are. But your children that you have fathered after them shall be yours, they shall be called by the names of their brothers in their inheritance."[209]

"What does that mean exactly?"

"The language used here is a form of adoption, similar to placing a child upon the knee as we've seen before. Jacob mentions Joseph's sons on the level of his own, perhaps implying they'll receive an inheritance of equal or even greater value than his own children. He goes on to groan about Rachel's premature death in this dialogue, a loss from which he never recovered, so it's possible the adoption is an expression of desire for the additional sons his favorite wife never had."

"This certainly falls in line with the ongoing theme of screwing up the inheritance order."

"It does indeed," said the man, reading on again:

When Israel saw Joseph's sons, and said, "Who are these?"

Joseph said to his father, "They are my sons, whom God has given me here."

And he said, "Bring them to me, please, that I may bless them."

Now the eyes of Israel were dim with age, so that he could not see.[210]

"Uh-oh," said the boy. "I sense a parallel with Isaac coming."

"Very good," said the man, reading on:

And Joseph brought them close to him, and he kissed them and embraced them. And Israel said to Joseph, "I never expected to see your face, and behold, God has let me see your children as well!"

Then Joseph took them from his knees, and bowed with his face to the ground. And Joseph took them both, Ephraim with his right hand toward Israel's left, and Manasseh with his left hand toward Israel's right, and brought them close to him.[211]

"Perfect," said the boy. "And the oldest will receive his proper blessing and we'll be on our merry way."

The old man smiled as he said, "Israel stretches out his right hand and lays it on Ephraim's head, who was the younger, and his left hand on Manasseh's, and then he blesses them. But when Joseph sees that his father's right hand is on Ephraim he tries to remove it and place in on Manasseh's, saying:

> "Not so, my father, for this one is the firstborn. Put your right hand on his head."

> But his father refused and said, "I know, my son, I know. He also shall become a people, and he also shall be great, but truly his younger brother shall be greater than he, and his descendants shall become a multitude of nations."[212]

"Shocking," said the boy.

"Yes," said the man, "you'd think Joseph in all his favoritism amongst his older brothers, and surely knowing the story of his father's own blessing, might have seen this coming. But Jacob acts neither by mistake nor partial affection, but rather from divine inspiration that goes against tradition. This image of Jacob crossing his arms to reach the younger son with his right hand and the older son with his left paints the summary of the Book of Genesis perfectly."

"Sure does," said the boy. "It sure does."

"We had Abel above Cain, Abraham above his brothers, Isaac over Ishmael, Jacob over Esau, Joseph before Reuben, and now Ephraim before Manasseh. God often gives the most to those that are least likely to have it," said the man, "chooses the weak to prosper, raises the poor to be rich. He doesn't follow the order of nature, nor does He prefer those who might be fit to be preferred, but chooses as He sees necessary."

"So does Jacob have any blessing for his other sons, or was he like Isaac with only one?"

"He sure does," said the man. "He goes through and blesses each one of his sons, tying a prophecy of their future to the blessing. For the sake of time, I'll tell you things look better for Joseph and Judah than for Simeon and Levi, but I'm sure you could have guessed that on your own."

"Another shocker," said the boy.

"Yes, well, it seemed he wanted to make examples of those who drift toward evil, as to not inspire similar action in the future of the rest of his kin. And with Jacob's dying words, he asks to be buried in the cave with his fathers in the field of Ephron, where he buried Leah some unknown years before."

"I was wondering if she was going to get the Eve treatment," said the boy. "No surprise there either."

"Yes, well, the Scripture is all we have to go by in these regards. But as Jacob finished giving his command, he drew his feet up into his bed and breathed his last breath. Joseph falls on his father's face and weeps over him. Then he commands his servants to embalm his father, and so the physicians did so."

"Really?" said the boy. "Was this part of the Hebrew culture? I thought this was an Egyptian thing."

"Well the tradition was certainly Egyptian," said the man, "but my guess is that this was done because he had to be carried to Canaan. This would be a trek of days, and therefore preserving the body was necessary to prevent putrefaction."

"Ah, that makes sense," said the boy.

"Forty days were required for this," said the man, "and, out of a great respect for Joseph, even the Egyptians mourned him during this time. And when the time comes, Joseph speaks to Pharaoh and pleads permission to carry his father to the cave in Canaan and promises to return. Pharaoh tells him, 'Go up and bury your father, as he made you swear.' So Joseph goes to bury his father, along with all the servants of Pharaoh, all the elders of Egypt, and all of Jacob's house. Only the little ones with their flocks and herds were left behind."

"Ah yes," said the boy. "Collateral."

"Both chariots and horsemen accompany them along this journey, and there was a great gathering to honor and mourn Israel. And after their father was buried, Joseph and his brothers return to Egypt."

"What a beautiful way to end the story," said the boy.

The man smiled. "But when Joseph's brothers saw that their father was dead, they said, 'Perhaps Joseph will hate us, and may actually repay us for all the evil which we did to him.' So they sent messengers to Joseph with a message," said the man:

"Before your father died, he instructed us to say to you, 'Please forgive your brothers for the great wrong they did to you, for their sin in treating you so cruelly.' So we, the servants of the God of your father, beg you to forgive our sin."[213]

"Jeez," said the boy, "leave it to this family to come up with lies and trickery at a funeral."

"Yes, well, a guilty conscience never rests," said the man, "and even when there is no danger it drums up fear and suspicion. But Joseph weeps when he hears this message, and when his brothers arrive before him they fall to their knees and bow, saying, 'Behold, we are your servants.' So here we have the fulfillment of the dream."

"So he rules over them after all," said the boy.

"Well, that was certainly the brothers' interpretation when a young Joseph first sought help finding its meaning. But here we see what an older Joseph discovers the meaning to be. He tells them this," said the man:

> "Don't be afraid. Am I in the place of God? You intended to harm me, but God intended it for good to accomplish what is now being done, the saving of many lives. So then, don't be afraid. I will provide for you and your children."[214]

"So he views it as taking care of them through the famine," said the boy.

"Precisely," said the man. "And so Joseph dwells in Egypt with the rest of his father's household and lives long enough to see his own grandchildren. But as he approaches the age of one hundred and ten years old, he tells his brothers, 'I am dying, but God will surely visit you, and bring you out of this land to the land of which He swore to Abraham, to Isaac, and to Jacob.' He hopes this will motivate them not to settle in Egypt, but rather encourage them to return to the promised land when the time comes. And with his dying words he commands an oath from the sons of Israel, saying, 'God will surely visit you, and you shall carry up my bones from here.' And then Joseph dies, being one hundred and ten years old, and they embalm him and he's placed in a coffin in Egypt. And here we see a story that began with God breathing life into His first creation come full circle in the end with the image of a chosen figure embalmed in a coffin." With that the man closed his Bible.

"We're done?" said the boy.

"We're done," said the man.

"Well, it certainly got a little weird at times," said the boy, "but overall not too shabby."

"I'm not sure *shabby* is the word I'd choose to describe the Holy Bible," said the man, "but I'm glad you could at least appreciate it."

"For sure," said the boy. "Lot of good takeaways."

"Indeed," said the man, "one of my favorites arriving in the story of Joseph, when we see who arises to the pinnacle of our tale. It is not those with inexcusable flaws or justified evil ways or pessimistic views, but rather he who sees positively and acts accordingly in times of chaos, who time and again lands on his feet and is elevated to the highest place in our story. Because Joseph is never resentful, nor bitter, nor malevolent, nor shaking his fist at God, he alone rises to become the shining symbol of the twelve tribes of Israel."

"And," said the boy, "he never ratted out his brothers again. Which to me means the real lesson of Genesis is don't be such a fuckin' tattletale."

The man shook his head with a laugh and said, "Why am I not surprised?"

Do you have a minute to support the author with a review?

END NOTES

[1] Gen. 2:24 (NKJV)

[2] Gen. 3:1-5 (NKJV)

[3] Gen. 3:7 (NJKV)

[4] Gen. 3:8-11 (ESV)

[5] Gen. 3:14-19 (NKJV)

[6] Gen. 3:21-24 (NASB)

[7] Gen 3:15 (NKJV)

[8] Robert Alter's *Genesis: Translation and Commentary*, W. W. Norton & Company. Kindle Edition.

[9] Gen. 4:6-7 (CSB)

[10] Gen. 4:8 (Robert Alter's *Genesis: Translation and Commentary*, W. W. Norton & Company. Kindle Edition.)

[11] Gen. 4:9-10 (NKJV)

[12] Gen. 4:11-12 (NKJV)

[13] Gen. 4:13-14 (NKJV)

[14] Gen. 4:15 (NKJV)

[15] Gen. 4:16-17 (Robert Alter's *Genesis: Translation and Commentary*, W. W. Norton & Company. Kindle Edition.)

[16] Gen. 4:23-24 (CSB)

[17] Gen. 6:5-6 (CSB)

[18] Gen. 6:7-8 (NKJV)

[19] Gen. 9: 22-25 (NASB)

[20] Gen 11: 3-4 (NKJV)

[21] Gen 11: 5-8 (CSB)

²² Gen. 12: 1-3 (NIV)

²³ Gen. 12: 10-13 (NIV)

²⁴ Gen. 12: 14-15 (ESV)

²⁵ Gen. 12: 18-20 (CSB)

²⁶ Gen. 13: 1-4 (NKJV)

²⁷ Gen 13. 5-7 (NASB)

²⁸ Gen 13. 8-9 (NKJV)

²⁹ Gen. 13:10 (NLT)

³⁰ Gen. 13:12-13 (NIV)

³¹ Gen. 14: 22-24 (ESV)

³² Gen. 15:1-3 (NKJV)

³³ Gen. 15:4-6 (NKJV)

³⁴ Gen. 15:12-13 (NKJV)

³⁵ Gen. 15:17 (NKJV)

³⁶ Gen. 16:3 (NKJV)

³⁷ Gen. 16:5 (NLT)

³⁸ Gen. 16:7-9 (NKJV)

³⁹ Gen. 16:11-12 (NKJV)

⁴⁰ Gen. 16:13 (NKJV)

⁴¹ Gen. 17:1-3 (NKJV)

⁴² Gen. 17:4-5 (NKJV)

⁴³ Gen. 17:10 (NKJV)

⁴⁴ Gen. 17:15-16 (NKJV)

⁴⁵ Gen. 17:17 (NASB)

⁴⁶ Gen. 17:19-20 (NASB)

⁴⁷ Gen. 17:23 (CSB)

⁴⁸ Gen. 18:2-5 (NASB)

⁴⁹ Gen. 18:7-9 (NKJV)

[50] Gen. 18:9-14 (NKJV)

[51] Gen. 18:16-19 (NIV)

[52] Gen. 18:20-21(NIV)

[53] Gen. 18:22-26 (NKJV)

[54] Gen. 18:27-29 (NKJV)

[55] Gen. 19:1-2 (CSB)

[56] Gen. 19: 4-5 (NKJV)

[57] Gen. 19:6-8 (NIV)

[58] Gen. 19:9-11 (NKJV)

[59] Gen. 19:12-14 (NKJV)

[60] Gen. 19:15 (NKJV)

[61] Gen. 19:16-17 (NLT)

[62] Gen. 19:18-19 (NIV)

[63] Gen. 19:21-22 (ESV)

[64] Gen. 19:23-26 (NASB)

[65] Gen. 19:31-32 (NKJV)

[66] Gen. 19:33-34 (NKJV)

[67] Gen. 19:35-38 (NKJV)

[68] Gen. 20:2 (NKJV)

[69] Gen. 20:2-3 (NKJV)

[70] Gen. 20:4-5 (NKJV)

[71] Gen. 20:6-7 (NKJV)

[72] Gen. 20:8-9 (NKJV)

[73] Gen. 20:10 (NIV)

[74] Gen. 20:11(NASB)

[75] Gen. 20:12 (NKJV)

[76] Gen. 20:13-14 (ESV)

[77] Gen. 20:15-16 (ESV)

[78] Gen. 20:17-18 (NKJV)

[79] Gen. 21:2-4 (ESV)

[80] Gen. 21:5-8 (ESV)

[81] Gen. 21:9-10 (NASB)

[82] Gen. 21:11-13 (NLT)

[83] Gen. 21:14 (ESV)

[84] Gen. 21:16-19 (NIV)

[85] Gen. 21:20-21 (NASB)

[86] Gen. 21:22-23 (NIV)

[87] Gen. 22:1-2 (ESV)

[88] Gen. 22:3-4 (NIV)

[89] Gen. 22:5-6 (CSB)

[90] Gen. 22:7 (NKJV)

[91] Gen. 22:8 (NIV)

[92] Gen. 22: 11-12 (NKJV)

[93] Gen. 22:13-14 (NKJV)

[94] Gen. 22:15-18 (NKJV)

[95] Gen. 24:1-2 (NKJV)

[96] Gen. 24:3-4 (NKJV)

[97] Gen. 24:5-8 (CSB)

[98] Gen. 24:9-10 (NKJV)

[99] Gen. 24:10-11 (NKJV)

[100] Gen. 24:12-15 (NKJV)

[101] Gen. 24:16-18 (NKJV)

[102] Gen. 24:21-23 (ESV)

[103] Gen. 24:24-27 (NASB)

[104] Gen. 24: 47-49 (NIV)

[105] Gen. 24:50-51 (NASB)

106 Gen. 24:63-67 (ESV)

107 Gen. 25:27-28 (ESV)

108 Gen. 25:29-34 (NKJV)

109 Gen. 27:1-4 (ESV)

110 Gen. 27:5-10 (NLT)

111 Gen. 27:11-14 (NIV)

112 Gen. 27:15-17 (NASB)

113 Gen. 27:18-20 (ESV)

114 Gen. 27:24-29 (NKJV)

115 Gen. 27:30-33 (NIV)

116 Gen. 27:34-35 (NIV)

117 Gen. 27:36-37 (ESV)

118 Gen. 27:38-40 (NIV)

119 Gen. 27:41-42 (ESV)

120 Gen. 27:42-45 (NIV)

121 Gen. 27:46 (NKJV)

122 Gen. 28:10 (NKJV)

123 Gen. 28:8-9 (NKJV)

124 Gen. 28:13-15 (NIV)

125 Gen. 28:16-18 (NKJV)

126 Gen. 28:20-22 (NIV)

127 Gen. 29:4-6 (NKJV)

128 Gen. 29:7-10 (ESV)

129 Gen. 29:12-14 (NASB)

130 Gen. 29:18 (NKJV)

131 Gen. 29:19-21 (ESV)

132 Gen. 29:22-25 (ESV)

133 Gen. 29:25-26 (ESV)

134 Gen. 29:27-30 (ESV)

135 Gen. 27:32-35 (NKJV)

136 Gen. 30:2-5 (NKJV)

137 Gen. 30:6-8 (NKJV)

138 Gen. 30:9-14 (NKJV)

139 Gen. 30:15 (NKJV)

140 Gen. 30:16 (NKJV)

141 Gen. 3:16 (NKJV)

142 Gen. 4:6-7 (CSB)

143 Gen. 30:17-18 (NIV)

144 Gen. 30:19-21 (NIV)

145 Gen. 30:22 (NKJV)

146 Gen. 30:23-26 (NASB)

147 Gen. 30:29-30 (NIV)

148 Gen. 30:31-33 (ESV)

149 Gen. 30:37-43 (CSB)

150 Gen. 31:1-3 (CSB)

151 Gen. 31:14-16 (NASB)

152 Gen. 32:4-6 (NIV)

153 Gen. 33:1-2 (NLT)

154 Gen. 33:5-11 (ESV)

155 Gen. 34:1-3 (NKJV)

156 Gen. 34:8-10 (ESV)

157 Gen. 34:11-12 (NIV)

158 Gen. 34:14-17 (ESV)

159 Gen. 34:25 (NIV)

160 Gen. 34:26-29 (CSB)

161 Gen. 34:30-31 (NKJV)

162 Gen. 35:10-12 (ESV)

163 Gen. 35:20-22 (NKJV)

164 Gen. 37:7 (CSB)

165 Gen. 37:18 (CSB)

166 Gen. 37:19-22 (ESV)

167 Gen. 37:23-24 (NASB)

168 Gen. 37:25-27 (NIV)

169 Gen. 37:32-33 (NKJV)

170 Gen. 38:11 (ESV)

171 Gen. 38:15-18 (NKJV)

172 Gen. 38:27-29 (NIV)

173 Gen. 39:2-6 (NIV)

174 Gen. 39:6-7 (ESV)

175 Gen. 39:21-23 (NIV)

176 Gen. 40:1-4 (NIV)

177 Gen. 40:5-6 (NKJV)

178 Gen. 40:7 (NIV)

179 Gen. 40:8 (ESV)

180 Gen. 40:9-15 (ESV)

181 Gen. 40:16-19 (ESV)

182 Gen. 40:20-23 (NLT)

183 Gen. 41:1-8 (NLT)

184 Gen. 41:25-36 (NIV)

185 Gen. 41:39-41 (ESV)

186 Gen. 42:13-16 (NIV)

187 Gen. 42:36 (NIV)

188 Gen. 42:37 (ESV)

189 Gen. 43:1-2 (ESV)

190 Gen. 43:3-7 (ESV)

191 Gen. 43:8-10 (NLT)

192 Gen. 43:11-14 (NKJV)

193 Gen. 43:27-29 (NASB)

194 Gen. 43:31-32 (NKJV)

195 Gen. 43:33 (NASB)

196 Gen. 44:4-9 (NIV)

197 Gen. 44:16 (NLT)

198 Gen. 44:17 (NKJV)

199 Gen. 45:1-5 (NKJV)

200 Gen. 46:3-4 (NKJV)

201 Gen. 46:5-6 (NKJV)

202 Gen. 47:9 (NKJV)

203 Gen. 47:13-16 (CSB)

204 Gen. 47:18-19 (NIV)

205 Gen. 47:20-22 (NLT)

206 Gen. 47:23-26 (NKJV)

207 Gen. 47:27-28 (NASB)

208 Gen. 47:29-31 (ESV)

209 Gen. 48:3-6 (NASB)

210 Gen. 48:8-10 (ESV)

211 Gen. 48:10-13 (NASB)

212 Gen. 48:18-19 (NKJV)

213 Gen. 50:16-17 (NLT)

214 Gen. 50:19-21 (NIV)

Made in the USA
Columbia, SC
24 June 2023

18661266R00150